SEMINAR STUDIES IN HISTORY

General Editor: Roger Lockyer

The Russian Revolution

Second Edition

Anthony Wood

LONGMAN
London and New York

LONGMAN GROUP UK LIMITED
Longman House, Burnt Mill, Harlow, Essex CM20 2JE, UK
and Associated Companies throughout the world.

Published in the United States of America
by Longman Inc., New York

First published 1979
Second edition 1986
Fourth impression 1989
ISBN 0 582 35559 1

Set in 10/11pt Linotron Baskerville
Produced by Longman Group (FE) Limited
Printed in Hong Kong

British Library Cataloguing in Publication Data

Wood, Anthony, *1923–*
    The Russian Revolution. – 2nd ed. – (Seminar studies in history)
    1. Soviet Union – History – Nicholas II, 1894–1917   2. Soviet
    Union – History – Revolution, 1917–1921   3. Soviet Union –
    Politics and government – 1894–1917   4. Soviet Union – Politics
    and government – 1917–1936
    I. Title   II. Series
    947.08′3   DK258

    ISBN 0–582–35559–1

Library of Congress Cataloging in Publication Data

Wood, Anthony.
    The Russian revolution.
    (Seminar studies in history)
    Bibliography: p.
    Includes index.
    1. Soviet Union – History – Revolution, 1917–1921.
    I. Title.   II. Series.
    DK265.W62   1986   947.084′1   85–19717
    ISBN 0–582–35559–1

Contents

Contents

Seminar Studies in History
Founding Editor: Patrick Richardson

Introduction

The Seminar Studies series was conceived by Patrick Richardson, whose experience of teaching history persuaded him of the need for something more substantial than a textbook chapter but less formidable than the specialised full-length academic work. He was also convinced that such studies, although limited in length, should provide an up-to-date and authoritative introduction to the topic under discussion as well as a selection of relevant documents and a comprehensive bibliography.

Patrick Richardson died in 1979, but by that time the Seminar Studies series was firmly established, and it continues to fulfil the role he intended for it. This book, like others in the series, is therefore a living tribute to a gifted and original teacher.

Note on the System of References:
A bold number in round brackets (**5**) in the text refers the reader to the corresponding entry in the Bibliography section at the end of the book. A bold number in square brackets, preceded by 'doc.' [**doc. 6**] refers the reader to the corresponding item in the section of Documents, which follows the main text.

ROGER LOCKYER
General Editor

Acknowledgements

We are grateful to the following for permission to reproduce copyright material:

Joel Carmichael for an extract from *The Russian Revolution 1917, A Personal Record* by N. Sukhanov, edited and translated by Joel Carmichael (1955); Lawrence & Wishart Ltd for extracts from *The Essentials of Lenin* Vol. II (1947); Macmillan London & Basingstoke for an extract from *The Russian Revolution* Vol. II (1935) by W. H. Chamberlain; Oxford University Press for extracts from *What is to be Done?* by Lenin, edited and translated by S. V. & P. Utechin (1965); Martin Secker & Warburg Ltd for an extract from *Izbrannye Sochineniya* Vol. III by Peter Tkachev, translated by T. Szamuely in *The Russian Tradition* (1974); Stanford University Press for extracts from *The Bolshevik Revolution 1917–1918* by James Bunyan & H. H. Fisher, Copyright © 1934 by the board of Trustees of the Leland Stanford Junior University, copyright renewed 1961 by James Bunyan & H. H. Fisher.

We have unfortunately been unable to trace the copyright owners of an extract from the private papers of Countess Sollohub from an article entitled 'A Visit to Butyrki Prison, Moscow' in *The National Review* Vol. 100 No. 603, May 1933, and would appreciate any information which would enable us to do so.

Cover: Lenin's arrival in Petrograd, April 1917. Mansell Collection, London.

Foreword

Most revolutions have been haphazard, the participants seizing their chance when it came, and the Russian revolution of 1917, which gave birth to the present Soviet regime, is in certain respects no exception to this. It is, however, unique in that it was preceded by decades of heated argument among left-wing groups of exiles over the form that it should eventually take and over the relation of their various social philosophies to the immediate tactics to be employed. This strange dialogue between intellectual theory and political action was to continue for some years after the Bolshevik coup, and the purpose of this book is to trace the thread of that dialogue from the years before the fall of the Tsarist monarchy up to the propounding of the New Economic Policy by Lenin in 1921. It is an immensely complicated story. A sketch of this length can naturally do no more than touch on some of the principal themes, but I hope that it may be helpful for the student to have an introductory outline from which he can move on to the many detailed studies that have already appeared.

The Tsarist calendar was thirteen days behind that of the west. To give both dates seemed tiresome, and since the subject is largely Russian domestic history, I have used the unreformed style until it was brought into line with the west at the end of January 1918. Names can also be confusing. I though it simpler and clearer to call Lenin's party the Bolsheviks throughout, although Lenin officially changed this to Communist on 8 March 1918. On the other hand, the left-wing members of the party, who emerged as a faction after the October revolution, are always known as the Left Communists and I have referred to them as that. Place-names, too, have changed. St. Petersburg became Petrograd in 1914 and finally settled down as Leningrad, just as Tsaritsyn was later to be Stalingrad, although more recent vicissitudes have now turned this into Volgograd.

Acknowledgements appear on a separate page, but I would like to take this opportunity of thanking my colleague Count Sollohub for permitting me to make use of an extract from his mother's memoirs for inclusion in the Documents section. My thanks are also due to my daughter Liisa who helped me with the preparation of the maps, and to my wife who is now confirmed in her dislike of all revolutions.

Note to the second edition

I have taken advantage of this second edition to expand the text slightly in places and to make some additions to the bibliography.

Part One: The Background

1   The setting

Tsarist Russia

The empire of Tsar Nicholas II, which was to be the scene of revolution in 1917, stretched across the vast expanse of European Russia and beyond the Urals to the sparsely populated plains of Siberia and the Far East. Even at the end of the nineteenth century this was still predominantly an agricultural country, and the two main features of Russian society were a hereditary class of slightly more than a million landed nobility and a peasantry who by the census of 1897 numbered 97 million out of a total population of approximately 110 million.

Until 1861 the majority of these peasants had been serfs who had maintained themselves by farming strips of their lords' land in return for labour service or a money payment, but with the emancipation of that year a portion of the landowners' estates had been made over to them – rather more than half in the poorer districts, considerably less in the rich black earth region of the south. Each village commune, which was the centre of peasant life, was to hold its allocation of this land in collective ownership. Thus, since the state had initially supplied the bulk of the financial compensation received by the landowners, the commune was made responsible for the repayment of this debt to the government in annual redemption dues over the subsequent forty-nine years, and within the commune the individual peasant paid his share of these dues according to the number of scattered strips allotted to his household at meetings of the village elders (**52**).

Although the abolition of serfdom was rightly hailed as a great reform, it did not end the separate legal status of the peasant within Russian society. The communal responsibility for the redemption payments also meant that until their abolition in 1905 he was as tied to the commune as he had been formerly to his master, and the more enterprising peasant who wished to clear his redemption debt and to extend and consolidate his holdings was often obstructed by the need for the consent of two-thirds of the village assembly. Still, by 1905 it was reckoned that one-tenth of the peasantry – the richer farmers known as the kulaks – held about a third of the commune land, and since some of these were able to buy or rent additional fields from the local nobility, the peasantry as a whole were farming about three-quarters of all the cultivable land available. Even this, however, was inadequate to resolve two further difficulties. First, unscientific methods and poor equipment on the open fields made it difficult to gain a yield sufficient to meet a heavy burden of taxation and redemption dues. Second, the enormous growth of the peasant population in the last half of the nineteenth century naturally created a land hunger within the areas controlled by the communes. The number of poor farmers and landless agricultural labourers was steadily rising and although the Stolypin reforms after 1906 (see p. 21) eased the problem a little, the estates of the Crown, the Orthodox Church and the nobility were to be a tempting prize, once public order had begun to break down after the revolution of February 1917 (**50**).

The middle class of professional men and merchants had always been small in Russia and still amounted to little more than half a million in 1897. In the last decades of the nineteenth century, however, a remarkable industrial growth suggested that Russia was beginning to move towards a western type of economy. Between 1875 and 1913 the output of coal multiplied some fourteen times, that of pig-iron some nine times. Much of this was stimulated by an immense railway boom which had brought the total length of track from 1,626 kilometres in 1860 to 30,539 kilometres by 1890, and in the following year work began on the building of the Trans-Siberian railway. The most rapid development was in the oil industry in the Caucasus, where output increased five times in the twenty years after 1885 (**42**).

The state gave encouragement to all this expansion, particularly while Count Sergei Witte was minister of finance from 1892 to 1903. Industry was protected by tariffs; domestic loans were floated; the government invested from national revenue and 67 per cent of Russian railways were state-owned by 1904. The shortage of capital, however, remained the major difficulty. Accordingly, in 1897 Witte put the rouble on the gold standard as a means of attracting money from abroad and by 1914 some 2,000 million roubles of foreign capital had been invested in Russia.

By the turn of the century there were perhaps some three million industrial workers, still only a tiny proportion of the total population. The primitive processes in many of the industries made them highly labour-intensive and demanded the concentration of great numbers of workers in large units of production – particularly in mining and metallurgy. At this stage of her industrial revolution Russia reflected many of the characteristics of a similar development earlier in western Europe. A law of 1897 had restricted the adult working day to eleven and a half hours and a somewhat ineffective system of factory inspection had been set up, but working and living conditions in the slums of the cities were often appalling and trade unions and strikes were still illegal.

This economic and social backwardness was matched by a system of government that lacked all the constitutional refinements of the west. It consisted of an autocracy exercised by the Tsar through the army, the police and the bureaucracy. The position of the monarchy was buttressed by the Russian Orthodox Church and by the loyalty of the land-owning nobility, from whom the main executive posts were filled, and the decrees of the Tsar were passed down from his ministers, whom he could appoint and dismiss at will, to provincial governors and town commandants in the large cities.

The period of reform in the reign of Alexander II (1855–81) had brought about some minor modification of this. An element of popular representation in local government had been introduced, when elective assemblies were set up at district and provincial levels in thirty-four provinces of European Russia. The system of voting for the district *zemstvos*, as they were called, was based on the class divisions in Russia, in that the nobles, townspeople and peasantry each chose their own representatives in separate electoral colleges, the peasantry by three stages; the provincial *zemstvos* were elected by the district assemblies. These bodies were allowed to raise their own revenue and were responsible for matters such as health, prisons and schools, but much of their activity was supervised by the bureaucracy. In 1870 a similar arrangement was extended to the cities which were granted the right to elect municipal councils, the franchise being based on a property qualification. These then appointed a mayor and an executive committee, who would concern themselves with local administration, although the choice of mayor had to be confirmed by the minister of the interior who also retained control over their police.

In addition to this, Alexander II had attempted to modernize the judicial system, and by a decree in 1864 a regional court was established in each province to deal with civil and criminal cases. Judges, appointed by the minister of justice, were to be irremovable, and trials were to be by jury and to be heard in public. All this only affected a small section of the population, since the separate legal status of the peasantry meant that they were answerable to their own *volost* court. At a district level, however, justices of the peace, elected by the *zemstvos*, were to deal with minor offences which did include cases involving the peasantry.

Naturally the reformers had hoped that these changes might be a prelude to the eventual establishment of a constitutional monarchy, but the only developments in the reign of Alexander III (1881–94) pointed in the other direction. In 1889 the position of justice of the peace was largely abolished and replaced by a land commandant, usually a civic official or a military or naval officer, who could exercise considerable control over the *volost* court and the communes. The powers of the *zemstvos*, too, were greatly restricted, and peasant representation in them was reduced, while in the cities the property qualification for the electors of the municipal councils was raised. In this atmosphere the likelihood of achieving the ultimate aim – the establishment of a parliamentary institution at a national level – appeared utterly remote.

Clearly much would depend upon the personality of the new Tsar who succeeded Alexander III in 1894 at the age of twenty-six. Nicholas II was a man of great personal charm, deeply religious and devoted to his family (**90**). He could be resolute, as he had shown when he had insisted upon marrying Princess Alix of Hesse-Darmstadt against the initial objections of his father. Unfortunately this quality of determination was marred by a sensitivity that inhibited him from openly opposing views with which he disagreed, and his ministers and officials could never be sure of his genuine acceptance of their advice, nor even of their own tenure of office. On one issue, at least, Nicholas did not leave them long in doubt. At the beginning of his reign the provincial *zemstvo* of Tver addressed an appeal to him for an extension of representative institutions. 'I am informed', said Nicholas in his reply, 'that recently in some *zemstvo* assemblies voices have made themselves heard from people carried away by senseless dreams about participation by representatives of the *zemstvo* in the affairs of internal government; let all know that I, devoting all my strength to the welfare of the people, will uphold the principle of autocracy as firmly and as unflinchingly as my late unforgettable father.' For Nicholas the autocracy was sacrosanct, a responsibility divinely entrusted to him, and the note of finality in his statement created an obstacle for the reformers that was to frustrate them until the last hours of the monarchy.

The Antecedents of Russian Revolutionary Thought

The vigilance of the Tsarist police in defence of the autocracy had given a special flavour to the political movements at work in Russia throughout the nineteenth century. They had had to be carried on in an atmosphere of conspiracy, and since their exponents lacked any practical experience in government, they tended towards an intellectual theorizing which was often radical and Utopian. In the main there were two general bodies of ideas, each inspired by a different response to the peculiar character of Russian history (**31**). The first of these demanded that Russia should shed her strange semi-Asiatic past and attempt to catch up with the west. The westernizers conceived this largely in technological terms – hence their liking for Peter the Great; they were not necessarily concerned with western types of constitutional development, although their attitude clearly influenced later Liberals who hoped for the growth of a parliamentary system of government. The second current of thought, known as Slavophil, strongly opposed any emulation of the west. The Slavophils regarded western institutions as alien to the spirit of Russia and they placed an almost mystical faith in the Russian peasant whose communal system of village life suggested the true foundation on which the future for Russia must rest.

Among the first to give intellectual shape to these vague aspirations in Russia was Alexander Herzen, originally a westernizer who emigrated to Paris and thence to London, grew disillusioned with what he saw there, and in 1857 began publishing his periodical *The Bell*, in which he sought to dissuade Russians from succumbing to the insidious example of the west. Initially Herzen made a considerable impact on the restless generations growing up in the 1860s and their response was to be seen in the Populist movement which dreamed of the liberation of the peasantry in a democratic Socialist society.

This was not to be based on any western model. The Populists believed that Russia must find a solution in harmony with her peasant institutions. Their vision of the future was a multiplicity of independent communes, each concerned with its own local industry and agriculture, and sufficiently small for the inhabitants to be saved from the depersonalizing effects of working in vast factories. They hated the thought of a monolithic state power and they maintained that once the revolution had occurred, the state would automatically wither away, although they were unsure of the precise stages by which this would happen. Despite these revolutionary objectives, however, most of the Populists maintained that the great transformation must come in its own time as a spontaneous manifestation of the will of the peasantry. Until then they intended simply to concentrate on propaganda and under Peter Lavrov and Nikolai Chaikovsky associations of university students were formed to encourage the dissemination of their ideas (**40**).

This patient approach did not appeal to all Populists and throughout the 1860s a far more extreme wing of the movement, known as Russian Jacobins, produced a highly significant series of statements (**38**). In September 1861 there was a proclamation by Mikhail Mikhailov, in 1862 a manifesto entitled *Young Russia* by Peter Zaichnevsky, in 1863 a novel *What is to be done?* by Nikolai Chernyshevsky, in 1868 *A Programme of Revolutionary Action* by Sergei Nechaev, followed later by *A Revolutionary Catechism*, and in 1874 *The Tasks of Revolutionary Propaganda in Russia* written by Peter Tkachev in Zürich (**41**). These spokesmen, who mostly died in prison or in exile, were not an organized group. Nevertheless, although the points that they stressed varied a little, there is an extraordinary consistency in their doctrine which combined fanaticism with a cold realism. Essentially they conceived a leadership in the hands of a small élite of professional revolutionaries; for Chernyshevsky these would be men of a totally superior type, puritanical and disciplined in their dedication to the cause; in Nechaev's *Catechism* they could employ any means with utter ruthlessness to attain their ends. 'Hard with himself, he must be hard with others.' The aim of this élite should be to inspire an immediate revolution in which the peasantry would overthrow the existing regime. There was to be no waiting for spontaneity, since this might entail so long a delay that a western type of capitalism would become strongly entrenched in Russia, bringing with it the destruction of the peasant commune. Furthermore, the state would not wither away as soon as the revolution had been accomplished, since the ruling élite would need the governmental apparatus as a means of enforcing the full realization of a Socialist society [**doc. 2**].

Lavrov hotly contested these views, which he declared could only lead to dictatorship, and for the moment the mainspring of Populist fervour remained a heady idealism. Its climax came in the summer of 1874, when swarms of university students calling themselves *Narodniki* – the men of the people – descended upon the peasantry in the countryside. Their aim was to preach the new gospel of liberation, but many of them seemed also to have had hopes of assimilating themselves with the peasantry, sharing the hardships and simplicity of their way of life. The outcome was almost total disillusionment. They discovered that the peasant was not the earthy saint that they had imagined; he was not even a Socialist and their efforts to improve his lot were only greeted with suspicion and derision.

Many of the *Narodniki* were arrested; the rest of them under the leadership of M. A. Natanson and George Plekhanov, the son of a small landowner, attempted in 1876 to set up a more formal organization, entitled 'Land and Liberty', whose aim was to encourage an insurrection which would give all land to the peasantry. Before long, however, sterner counsels had prevailed. Radicals in the party, despairing of any assistance from liberals in the *zemstvos*, demanded a policy of terrorism, to be carried out by a small group of dedicated revolutionaries. At a secret congress at Voronezh in 1879 Plekhanov and Paul Akselrod were unable to defeat these proposals; the terrorists now took over the movement, calling themselves the People's Will, and during the next few years built up an impressive record of assassination, including Tsar Alexander II in 1881.

Shortly after this split Plekhanov and Akselrod withdrew into self-imposed exile in Geneva. They had by this time lost faith in the revolutionary potential of the Russian peasantry and with this abandonment of Populism turned instead to Marxism. Karl Marx was a German Jew who in 1849 had established himself in London, where he devoted the rest of his life to an analysis of the laws which governed the development of society. He was a man of immense erudition and intellectual power, who, although no politician himself, was a source of inspiration for most Socialist bodies of his day and before his death in 1883 he had seen the emergence of large Marxist Social Democrat parties in most western European countries (**36**).

It is, nevertheless, important to distinguish between Marx and Marxism. Although dogmatic in utterance, he preserved a remarkable flexibility in his ideas; principally he was concerned with a new way of looking at things, rather than with providing any rule-of-thumb solutions, and he was often appalled at the oversimplifications made by his followers. But mass movements do not thrive on intellectual subtleties and Marx himself rather added to the difficulties of interpretation by leaving a good deal of his major writings incomplete. *Capital* was only the first part of a much larger unfinished work, of which his associate Engels put together two further volumes after his death, and much else was not published until long after the Russian revolution.

Consequently Marxism is more important than Marx for an understanding of the Social Democrat movement. The fundamental thesis was that history was a process of change in which the structure of society depended upon the pattern of economic relations within it (**26, 37**). The key to the pattern was the control of the means of production by a particular social class, who could then use this to exploit the labour of all the rest. As one class became dominant, it would establish a superstructure of political, religious and cultural institutions reflecting its own interest and enjoying the protection of the state. The supremacy of this class, however, could never be permanent, since the growth of other factors would alter the economic basis on which its power rested, and this would lead to the emergence of a new class which would eventually take over from the previous one. Thus the course of history consisted of a continuing struggle in which separate classes gained power in a recognizable sequence [**doc. 1**].

It was Marx's knowledge of western Europe that had suggested this process. Here a feudal aristocracy, basing itself on land farmed with serf labour, had been dominant until, with the growth of a money economy, a bourgeois capitalist class had superseded it, finally consolidating its position in the English civil war and the French Revolution. This new class reinforced itself with forms of liberal democracy whose parliamentary institutions legislated on behalf of private property and made use of the state to fight capitalist wars and to gain empire in search of markets and raw materials. Eventually, however, this bourgeois predominance created the circumstances that would lead to its own collapse. Economic competition stimulated the growth of industry which brought into existence a large urban working class. This proletariat would soon become such a significant force in the system of production that the economic basis of bourgeois power would be undermined and the proletariat would then carry out their own revolution, probably at some moment when the rivalry of capitalist states had resulted in a vast war or an economic breakdown. There would then follow the dictatorship of the proletariat, which much later would usher in the final stage, the classless society. In this, no single section of the community would control the means of production. There would thus be no further need for the state, which would begin to wither away, and society would inscribe on its banner: 'From each according to his ability, to each according to his need'.

Although Marx was later beginning to modify his views, his followers were convinced that the sequence was inexorable. For societies which had reached the bourgeois stage it was futile to hope that efforts to alleviate the harshness of the capitalist system through welfare legislation, charitable institutions or trade union negotiations could hold up the historical process; bourgeois society was bound to succumb to the proletarian revolution. Equally, it would be disastrous to run ahead of schedule. The bourgeois had to seize power first and the proletarian revolution could only follow after industrialization had been established long enough for the working class to be ready for the next step. To act prematurely by stimulating a proletarian revolution before the circumstances were ripe for it would only invite heroic defeat on the barricades, or, at the most, establish a revolutionary clique grimly clinging to power in a short-lived dictatorship. Thus the duty of the Marxist was to prepare the proletariat for their eventual role, to judge the correct moment for the revolution and then to assume the leadership when it ensued.

It was natural that this apparently scientific analysis should appeal to Russian Socialists who had become disillusioned with Populism. To Plekhanov and Akselrod in Geneva it offered a clear philosophy in which the working class, now emerging with Russia's rapidly growing industrialization, were the key to the future (**76**). In 1883 they founded the Emancipation of Labour group which by the 1890s had fostered a number of circles of Marxist Social Democrats in the industrial centres of Russia. They were aided by the fact that the Tsarist censorship had allowed the publication of Marx's *Capital*, translated in 1872, and of other Marxist writings; but any political activity was prohibited and the meeting of the first congress of the Russian Socialist Democrat Workers' Party at Minsk in 1898 was followed almost at once by the arrest of most of the delegates.

This was not the principal difficulty. Social Democrats in western Europe could reckon that the capitalist stage was sufficiently far advanced there for them to be able to work directly for the proletarian revolution. Russia, however, had yet to accomplish her bourgeois revolution. This meant that her proletarian revolution must still be many years distant – not a very exciting prospect – and Plekhanov, who was by now the father figure of Russian Marxism, was faced with the question of the role to be played by the relatively

small Russian proletariat in the meantime. In fact, Marx himself
had opened up an interesting speculation on this matter. For most
of his life he had opposed the ideas of the Populists, but in 1881
he suggested that the institution of the commune and the degree
of revolutionary fervour in Russia might make an immediate
Socialist revolution possible there, provided that it was
accompanied by other revolutions in the west. This was a theory
that was to be extremely significant in the Bolshevik decision to
seize power in 1917 (see p. 38), but for the moment it did not enter
into Plekhanov's calculations. His solution was that the Russian
working class should support the Liberals in their bourgeois
revolution, but must remain sufficiently detached in their organization to preserve their own later political goal, and in this respect
he proved himself a more orthodox Marxist than his master.

Russian Political Groups at the Beginning of the Twentieth Century

At the turn of the century the autocracy in Russia was confronted
with a series of student demonstrations, industrial strikes and
peasant outbreaks. This unrest gave great encouragement to a
variety of political aspirations, all of which derived from the
ferment of ideas in earlier years. Very roughly, it is possible to
identify three main groups – Liberals, Social Revolutionaries and
Social Democrats – within each of which, however, there was a
considerable range of opinion.

(a) LIBERALS

The word Liberal at this point in Russian history sums up the hope
for constitutional reform and political liberty. This westernizing
tradition in Russian thought was to be found among politicians and
administrative officials of the *zemstvos*, in the universities and in
various professional associations, and in Marxist eyes they were the
class that should one day bring about the bourgeois revolution in
Russia, although only a few of them had any idea of taking power
by force.

The more conservative merely wanted an extension of the
consultative principle through some kind of *zemstvo* organization on
a national scale. In 1896, for example, D. N. Shipov, chairman of
the board of the Moscow *zemstvo*, arranged a meeting of the
chairmen of other provincial boards, and three years later managed
to persuade Goremykin, the minister of the interior, to extend the

zemstvos to the western regions of Russia and the lower Volga – a proposal which only led to Goremykin's dismissal. At the same time other groups of intellectuals and university teachers, who were not directly connected with the *zemstvo* movement, were more concerned with social reforms such as universal primary education and an end to the separate legal status of the peasantry.

The more radical wing of the Liberals demanded a fully fledged constitutional programme of a western type. They wanted a limited monarchy answerable to a parliament elected by direct universal suffrage, and they coupled the notion of democracy with 'a defence of the interests of the labouring masses' and the right of self-determination for the subject nationalities under Russian rule. Although these radical leaders did not intend open revolution, an opposition of this kind was bound to be illegal and at first could only operate from abroad. In 1901 they established a newspaper *Liberation* in Stuttgart; two years later at a meeting at Schaffhausen they formed a Union of Liberation which they hoped would appeal to all Liberals, and in January 1904 they drew up a manifesto of their aims at a meeting in St. Petersburg.

(b) SOCIAL REVOLUTIONARIES (S.R.)

The other two groups were purely conspiratorial and Socialist in aim. The Social Revolutionaries grew out of a revival of the Populist movement, when a number of veteran members of the People's Will returned in the 1890s from exile in Siberia. The name, the Union of Social Revolutionaries, first appeared in 1896 in Saratov; before long contact had been established with similar organizations in the south and at Minsk, and in 1901 Viktor Chernov set up a small combat detachment in Berlin designed to renew the policy of terror. In the following year a more broadly based political party was founded at Geneva, soon disseminating propaganda in Russia through its own newspaper, and in 1903 the Social Revolutionaries were admitted to the congress of the Second International (**32**). Eventually in 1906 they drew up a comprehensive programme, which stated as their maximum aim the creation of a fully Socialist society, while the interim minimum aims concentrated on the summoning of a Constituent Assembly which would set up a federal republic, guaranteeing political liberty and a separation of church and state (**39**).

It might seem that their common belief in Socialism should have drawn the Social Revolutionaries and the Russian Social Democrats into alliance. There were, however, several points of distinction that were always to keep them apart. Essentially the Social Revolutionaries were undoctrinaire. They envisaged a general revolutionary movement which would embrace all the discontented, and they were uninterested in the intellectual niceties of Marxism which attempted to define the successive stages of the class struggle. True to their Populist origins, they had no wish to see a vast industrial proletariat develop along western lines and they looked instead for an immediate transition to a decentralized mass of workers' cooperatives. Principally their attention was concentrated upon the peasantry. To them they promised all the land without compensation for the previous owners and they still dreamed of thousands of small peasant communities whose farming would be based on local collective ownership.

None of this was acceptable to the Marxism of the Russian Social Democrats. They argued that the growth of a vast industrial working class was an essential preliminary to the eventual Socialist revolution. Furthermore, they profoundly mistrusted the Social Revolutionaries' programme for the land. They believed that a system of small units would enable the more successful peasants to establish themselves as a wealthy class of capitalist farmers, and they insisted that this could only be averted by a policy of outright nationalization. Lastly, there was a difference of view over tactics, since the Marxists regarded terrorism as irrelevant to the unfolding of the historical process.

Thus any alliance between the two seemed unlikely. Indeed the Russian Social Democrats were soon made aware that they were faced with a formidable rival. Marxist doctrine suggested that any Socialist revolution in Russia would be long delayed, whereas the Social Revolutionaries offered immediate action and their Populist past give them great influence with the peasantry who warmed to the idea of gaining the land, without listening very much to the Socialist aspect of the programme.

(c) RUSSIAN SOCIAL DEMOCRATS: BOLSHEVIKS AND MENSHEVIKS
While the Social Revolutionaries were giving new expression to Populist ideals, the Social Democrat movement was facing an internal crisis of its own. In 1899 a German Social Democrat, Eduard Bernstein, had challenged the central feature of Marxism, when he declared that the working class should cease to aim at revolutionary action and should merely fight for their cause through trade unions and existing parliamentary processes. This revisionism, as it was called, was particularly upsetting for

orthodox Marxists in the west, where they reckoned that the moment for the proletarian rising was approaching. It seemed less relevant to Russia who was still awaiting her bourgeois revolution, but even here a group of Russian Social Democrats, known as Economists, were advocating their own type of modification, when they insisted upon a specialization of functions within the party. The political leadership was to be exclusively in the hands of intellectuals, who should assist the Liberal opposition, while the proletariat should rely purely upon improving their conditions at work through their trade union organizations.

It is open to question how far the Economists were directly attacking the fundamental precepts of Marxism, but to Plekhanov in Geneva their policy appeared utterly heretical. Like those who condemned Bernstein, he believed that a concentration on trade union activity would simply make the proletariat a subordinate element in the development of Russian capitalism and that they would thus lose their identity as a separate revolutionary force in the class struggle. Indeed, there was already evidence in Russia that suggested that he was right to scent danger. In St. Petersburg a senior police official, Sergei Zubatov, had also seen that trade unionism might provide a means of quietening any revolutionary instincts among the Russian proletariat. He had accordingly devised a plan for setting up trade unions under police supervision, and as concessions were wrung from the employers, he hoped that this would strengthen a sense of loyalty to the Tsar who would be shown to be on the side of the workers. Zubatov at first had considerable success, but to conservative interests at court it seemed that his policy was aiding the cause of radicalism and in 1903 they secured his dismissal.

There was a further aspect of trade unionism which seemed likely to weaken the revolutionary unity of the workers. The first Social Democrat organizations to emerge among the working class in Russia were a large number of Jewish trade unions, which amalgamated in 1897 to form a *Bund*. Increasingly, however, they had come to concentrate on easing the position of Jews in Russia who suffered from the anti-Semitic attitudes of the government and local populations. This separateness of aim led them to demand autonomy within the Russian Social Democrat Party and it seemed to many outside the *Bund* that this exclusiveness could be divisive.

Consequently the question of trade unions loomed large in the minds of orthodox Russian Marxists at this time. Principally they were concerned to refute the doctrine of the Economists and they were to be aided in this by a new generation of young revolutionaries. Among these was Vladimir Ilyich Ulyanov, who later adopted the conspiratorial name of Lenin (**70–74**). Born in 1870, he was the son of a school inspector in the Volga region. Most of the children of the family had been influenced by the ideas of the Populists, and in 1887 Lenin's elder brother Alexander was hanged for taking part in a plot to assassinate Tsar Alexander III. Lenin's own university career had been interrupted on account of the suspicion of the authorities and he was only able to qualify in law as an external student in 1891. By now he had turned from Populism to the writings of Marx, and from 1893 he was involved in secret Social Democrat activities in St. Petersburg (**48**). Here in 1895 he met another young revolutionary, Julius Tsederbaum. Martov, as he was known, was a Jew from Odessa, whose conversion to Marxism had already earned him a short spell of imprisonment (**75**). These two now formed a Union of Struggle for the Emancipation of the Working Class, but by the end of the year they had been arrested and were deported to Siberia. There the conditions of life for political prisoners were sufficiently relaxed for Lenin to be able to continue his Marxist studies and even to write a book, *The Development of Capitalism in Russia*. At the same time he too had been alarmed at the growth of the Economist doctrine, and as soon as he was released in 1900, he made his way to Geneva in order to concert plans with Plekhanov for combating it.

The method which they adopted was to spread orthodox Marxist views through a newspaper, *Iskra*, which was to be written and printed in the relative freedom of the west and then smuggled into Russia for circulation among the Social Democrat groups. By the beginning of 1901 an editorial board of six had been set up – Plekhanov, Akselrod, and Vera Zasulich representing the older generation, together with Lenin, Martov and Potresov, an associate of their St. Petersburg days. The younger members of the board eventually established themselves in London and it was here in October 1902 that they were joined by Leon Bronstein – Trotsky – who had recently made his escape from Siberia (**79–83**). Like Lenin, Trotsky had not been prevented by his exile in Siberia from making a literary reputation for himself in Marxist circles, and his services were now so valuable to the *Iskra* group that only the opposition of Plekhanov stopped Lenin from making him a member of the board.

In 1902 Lenin bolstered up the campaign with a separate pamphlet entitled *What is to be done?* [**doc. 3**]. Although this continued the attack on the Economists, it did also reveal another idea in his mind which was eventually to bring about a split in the Russian Social Democrat movement far more significant than that created by the current controversy. The Economist doctrine had suggested that without firm control the working class could easily be led on to the wrong track and Lenin was now convinced that the party must have a disciplined unity under the leadership of a small élite of professional revolutionaries. He did not exclude freedom of debate; indeed, for many years his position rested largely upon his own power of argument, but he believed that once a decision had been reached, the rank and file must give an unquestioning obedience. This had little to do with Marx. It is significant that Lenin took the title of his pamphlet from Chernyshevsky's novel, and the principle that he enunciated was directly in the tradition of the Russian Jacobins, summed up by Tkachev, with whose work he was certainly familiar (**5**).

The issue came out into the open at the meeting of the second congress of the Russian Social Democrat party in July 1903. This was held at Brussels until the activity of the Belgian police eventually caused it to move to London. The purpose of the congress was to devise the programme and the statutes of the party. Among the forty-three voting delegates, the *Iskra* men were in the majority and this did enable them to defeat the Economists as well as the representatives of the *Bund* whose demand for autonomy within the party was rejected.

Before this, however, the *Iskra* men had already become divided over the definition of membership of the party. Lenin wanted it to be restricted to those who gave their support 'both materially and by personal participation in one of its organizations'. Martov wanted it to be open to those who supported it 'both materially and by regular cooperation under the leadership of one of its organizations' (**53**). The difference might seem slight, but it was none the less crucial. Lenin's formula pointed to a small revolutionary élite in control of the movement; Martov's reflected his genuine belief in a wider democratic appeal among all Socialists.

For the moment Lenin encountered defeat. The delegates were by this time suspicious of his dictatorial tendencies and uncompromising invective, and although he had the support of Plekhanov, they adopted Martov's version. Later the Economists and the *Bund* representatives withdrew from the congress and this swung the balance of the voting slightly in Lenin's favour. By this time it had been settled that there should be a central committee of three within Russia under the direction of a central organ outside Russia, the editorial board of *Iskra*. These two bodies were to elect four of the five members of a supreme party council and Lenin now returned to the attack, determined to fill these places with his own nominees. He proposed that the editorial board of *Iskra* should be reduced to three – Plekhanov, Martov and himself – and after his newly-found majority had enabled him to get his way, the congress broke up amid a violent altercation, with Martov vehemently refusing to serve on the new editorial board.

Lenin's victory was short-lived. By the end of the year Plekhanov had changed sides and brought back the old members of the board, whereupon Lenin resigned. The majority with which he had temporarily gained his ends at the congress had been no more than a chance circumstance; yet it was characteristic of him to retain the name *Bolsheviki* ('the men of the majority') for his faction; for the future Martov and the bulk of the Social Democrats were to remain the *Mensheviki* ('the men of the minority'). Lenin was determined that there should be no reconciliation and it was under these two flags that the groups of quarrelling émigrés were to continue their feud until it came to their attention at the beginning of 1905 that a revolution had actually broken out in Russia.

2 The Revolution of 1905 and its Consequences

The Course of the Revolution

The immediate background to the revolution of 1905 was the war that began early in the previous year between Russia and Japan over the control of Korea and Manchuria. The Japanese took possession of Korea almost at once and throughout the rest of 1904 concentrated their efforts on the siege of Port Arthur which finally surrendered at the beginning of 1905. They then advanced northwards through southern Manchuria and two months later defeated the Russians again at Mukden. Meanwhile, the Russian Baltic fleet had been sailing half way round the world to meet the enemy, but on its arrival in the straits of Tshushima towards the end of May it was virtually destroyed by the Japanese. This brought the war to a fairly decisive conclusion and at the peace signed in August 1905 Japan took over Korea and the southern half of Manchuria.

In Russia the early stages of the war had encouraged the various Liberal groups, including the illegal Union of Liberation, to press their demands for a representative system of government at a series of meetings and banquets. The principal act of violence in 1904 was the assassination of Plehve, the minister of the interior, by a Social Revolutionary, but after the fall of Port Arthur revolutionary outbreaks began to spread rapidly throughout the country (**44**).

The first episode occurred on 9 January 1905 – Bloody Sunday – when Father Gapon, a priest who had been allowed by the authorities to form a union of St. Petersburg factory workers, led a large demonstration to the Winter Palace to present a petition for the summoning of a constituent assembly. The troops opened fire on the crowd, causing the death of more than a hundred. This was followed at once by a general strike throughout St. Petersburg, the killing of officials and, on 4 February, the assassination of the governor-general of Moscow, Grand Duke Sergei, the Tsar's uncle. On 18 February Tsar Nicholas attempted to win over the Liberals by agreeing to the election of a consultative assembly, but by the spring peasant revolts had broken out in three provinces and continued to spread throughout the summer, a situation which the Social Revolutionaries did their best to exploit by organizing a national peasant congress. In June there was a mutiny at Odessa on the battleship *Potemkin*, whose crew eventually sailed her to Romania, while in the cities trade unions were rapidly being formed and university students were turning over their lecture halls for political meetings.

Against this background of upheaval the leaders of the *zemstvo* movement had combined with representatives from municipal councils and in July a draft constitution drawn up by a joint congress under Professor Milyukov went far beyond the Tsar's proposals for a merely consultative assembly. The troubles continued into the autumn, when on 8 October a new railway strike was followed by a general strike in most cities. Five days later the St. Petersburg Soviet (Council) of Workers' Deputies was formed; on 17 October this elected an executive committee with a lawyer Khrustalev-Nosar as president and Trotsky as vice-president, and before long the Soviet was pressing the demand for an eight-hour working day.

At this moment Tsar Nicholas was at last persuaded to take the steam out of the revolution by making further concessions. Count Witte, previously suspect on account of his reformist tendencies, was appointed premier, and an amnesty was announced, together with a manifesto promising a fuller constitution with an elective assembly – the Duma – whose consent would be necessary for all future laws. This did not satisfy all the Liberals, but at least it gave them a start. Among the workers, too, it seemed to offer a new hope and the St. Petersburg Soviet began to feel its own influence slipping away. Then early in November another manifesto attempted to mollify the peasantry by abolishing the redemption dues (see p. 1). The government was now free from the demands of war in the Far East and on 3 December Witte felt sufficiently confident to place the executive of the Soviet under arrest; a subsequent rising in Moscow was crushed by the Semenovsky Guards regiment, and although disorders continued throughout much of 1906, the government was slowly able to re-establish its authority.

In many ways the pattern of events had been similar to that of the central European revolutions of 1848 and the reasons for failure were roughly the same. Despite the defeats in the Russo-Japanese war the government had not lost control of its armed forces, and the mutinies at Sebastopol, Kronstadt and on the *Potemkin* had been isolated affairs. The Liberals were uneasy about the forces of violence by which they were borne along and had been content to settle for a constitution handed down to them from above. The workers and peasants had shown that they could create havoc, but their actions had been too haphazard to be effective, once the government had succeeded in dividing its opponents with the publication of the October manifesto.

Of the Socialist groups it was probably the Social Revolutionaries who achieved the most; in the course of the risings they were able to consolidate a hold on the peasantry which they still retained in 1917. The Social Democrats were distinctly less successful. Their underground committees in Russia had struggled to give shape to the workers' movements; in the Caucasus, for example, Joseph Stalin, as he later called himself, the son of a Georgian shoemaker, helped the strikers in the oil industry to beat off the attacks of the Black Hundreds, gangs of strike-breakers organized by the government. Yet the extraordinary feature of the Social Democrat performance is that throughout most of the revolution the leaders in exile still appeared more interested in their own factional struggle. As late as April 1905 Lenin was holding what he claimed was a Social Democrat party congress in London, where a new central committee, entirely Bolshevik, was elected – to which the Mensheviks responded by holding a conference of their own at Geneva.

Most of the émigré Social Democrats only arrived on the scene of events after the amnesty in the autumn of 1905 had made it safe to return to Russia. Neither the Mensheviks nor the Bolsheviks were responsible for the creation of the St. Petersburg Soviet which emanated largely from various factory committees. The Mensheviks under Martov saw the upheaval principally as a bourgeois revolution and were never able to define clearly the part that the proletariat should play in it. In fact, the only positive line of action came from Trotsky, who, aided by another Russian émigré, Alexander Helphand (Parvus) (**69**), was determined to use the Soviet as a force against the Liberals as well as the government. Lenin himself did not get to St. Petersburg until November 1905 and even then regarded the situation with some caution. He knew that his Bolshevik organization was not yet sufficiently developed to gain control and he was profoundly mistrustful of the Soviet, which, as an amalgam of many left-wing attitudes, was remote from his conception of a disciplined revolutionary body. Long afterwards he described the 1905 revolution as the great dress rehearsal, but at the time he does not seem to have considered it his play at all.

The Duma Period

The Tsar's promise of a national parliament was followed in February 1906 by a new manifesto announcing the details of the representative system. In the upper house – the Council of State – half the members were to be nominated and half to be elected by the *zemstvos* and the higher orders of society. The lower house – the Duma – was to consist of deputies elected by universal suffrage. Only the five largest cities would vote directly, the rest of the electorate indirectly through electoral colleges, the peasantry mostly by two stages. On 14 April, however, Witte was replaced by Goremykin and nine days later the hopes for full parliamentary government were shattered when the Tsar published the Funda-mental Laws defining the precise powers of the Duma. Ministers were to be solely responsible to the Tsar, and the Duma was to have no control over that part of the budget concerned with mili-tary and naval estimates, nor over the raising of foreign loans. Thus the Laws, which were not open to debate, made it clear that the new assembly's role was after all to be no more than consultative, since it would have no financial weapon with which to bring about a change of government.

Elections were already taking place and the first Duma met in the Tauride palace in St. Petersburg on 27 April 1906. The largest party consisted of 179 Constitutional Democrats – the Kadets – who under Milyukov had campaigned on a fairly radical programme; to the right were seventeen Octobrists under Shipov, so called because they were prepared to rest content with the October manifesto; to the left were ninety-four Trudoviki, a Labour group which included a number of Social Revolutionaries despite their party's decision not to participate; and eighteen Social Democrats, all Mensheviks and largely from Georgia.

The first Duma was hardly a success, principally because the Tsar was not prepared to appoint a government acceptable to the Kadets. These, meanwhile, were demanding a redistribution of the landowners' estates, and when this was rejected by Goremykin, they announced that any settlement of the land question must depend upon the consent of the Duma. Accordingly at the begin-ning of July Nicholas declared a dissolution and appointed Stolypin as premier in place of Goremykin. On this, half of the Duma deputies moved into Finland and issued an appeal for the refusal of taxes and recruits for the army until the dissolution had been rescinded. The general response was more violent than they had intended – sporadic peasant revolt, assassinations, and mutinies at Sveaborg and Kronstadt – and to restore order Stolypin established courts martial which by April 1907 had passed 683 sentences of death.

At the same time he was making arrangements for a new election, but the second Duma which met on 20 February 1907 proved no more amenable than the first. The extremes of left and right were more strongly represented – at the expense of the Kadets, who dropped to ninety-two seats; there ensued long attacks on the army, and eventually Stolypin, alleging that there was a plot against the Tsar's life by Social Democrats, dissolved the Duma on 3 June. The next step clearly was to revise the franchise in the interest of the landowners; the third Duma, elected under these new arrangements, was predominantly conservative and although there were occasional disagreements, this was to last from November 1907 until 1912, when it was succeeded by a fourth of similar composition (**45**).

Thus far, Stolypin might seem a convenient instrument for the Tsar whereby most of the concessions granted under the pressure of the revolution could be effectively nullified. That was certainly how many of the Liberals and the left saw him. Nevertheless, Stolypin's administration, which lasted until his assassination by a Social Revolutionary in September 1911, did gradually bring about a number of fundamental economic and social reforms. The *zemstvos*, aided by the central government, carried out a considerable extension of health services in the provinces and in 1912 a system of health insurance for workers was set up. In 1908 compulsory universal education within ten years became a declared aim; by 1914 the government had established 50,000 additional primary schools, administered and largely financed by the *zemstvos*, and there was also an expansion of institutions of higher and secondary education.

The most significant of all these changes was the land reforms. These were embodied in a series of laws whereby the peasant might become the owner of the scattered strips which he held from the village commune and which could now be rearranged so as to form consolidated farmsteads. As a consequence approximately half the number of peasant households held their land individually by 1915 and a sixth of these had been able to achieve some degree of consolidation. Shortage of land, due to the growing peasant population, remained a fundamental problem, but the government did try to ease this by encouraging migration to Siberia and other parts of the east, and credit facilities enabled the more enterprising to purchase parts of estates from the nobility. Peasant proprietorship clearly opened the way to the development of a class of farmer who would have a vested interest in the status quo and Lenin himself saw the danger that it represented for his hopes. 'If this should continue for long periods of time,' he wrote in 1908, '. . . it might force us to renounce any agrarian programme at all' (**83**).

There were two other difficulties as well that hampered the Socialist movement during these years. First, the Tsarist police became highly successful at infiltrating their organizations. Evno Azef, who until 1908 led the fighting section of the Social Revolutionaries, was a police agent; so, too, were two members of the editorial board of the Bolshevik *Pravda*, founded in 1912; another, Roman Malinovski, actually became a member of the Bolshevik central committee and, before suspicion finally closed in on him, was able to secure the arrest of Sverdlov and Stalin who were deported to Siberia in 1913.

Second, the Social Democrats, whose leaders had mostly returned to exile by 1907, were weakened by the continued feuding between Mensheviks and Bolsheviks over issues that were largely incomprehensible to their supporters in Russia. Doctrinally the Mensheviks were absolutely orthodox in their Marxism. They believed that Russia still awaited her bourgeois revolution and that the proletarian revolution could only come many years after that. To Lenin, however, the rapid growth of the proletariat and the general weakness of the bourgeois class in Russia suggested that the two revolutions could follow upon one another in rapid succession, provided that the peasantry were brought into active partnership with the proletariat as a revolutionary force. In this tangle of conflicting theory there was a third faction represented by Trotsky and Alexander Helphand, both of whom had escaped from Siberia after their deportation there in 1906. Trotsky disagreed with Lenin's conception of the disciplined party and of the role to be played by the peasantry. On the other hand, he did believe that the two revolutions could be combined, if they were accompanied by revolution elsewhere in Europe (**80**).

These were characteristically academic considerations. The more practical obstacle was that Lenin was determined to build up an entirely separate Bolshevik organization whose central committee would exercise absolute control over a network of small cells throughout Russia. When the Mensheviks declared that in the new circumstances of the Duma period the underground groups should come out into the open and work with the trade unions, which had been legalized in 1906, he denounced them as 'liquidators'. In reply the Mensheviks attacked his policy of swelling his funds by means of a series of bank robberies in Russia (**83**), and after a Bolshevik conference at Prague in January 1912, there seemed little likelihood of any reconciliation between the two factions.

The Impact of the Great War

In August 1914 Russia, in alliance with Great Britain and France, found herself at war with Germany and Austria-Hungary. The strain that this was to involve was an essential factor in the eventual outbreak of revolution in February 1917, although not precisely for the reasons that have sometimes been given.

It has been suggested, for example, that after the entry of Turkey on the side of the Central Powers in October 1914 had deprived Russia of a major supply route through the Straits, Russian industry was incapable of meeting the demand for munitions, and that by the beginning of 1917 the Russian army, dispirited and ill-equipped, was near to collapse. In fact, recent research has shown that shortages were due to administrative confusion rather than deficiences in production, and the 4.5 million shells that Russia was turning out per month by September 1916 compare well with the seven million of the Germans who were coping with war on two fronts (**51**). The army, too, far from being broken, had proved an effective force. It is true that they had been pushed back on to Russian soil, but there had been two successful offensives, into Austrian Galicia in 1914 and under Brusilov in 1916, and the Central Powers had in all suffered more casualties on the eastern front than they had in the west.

It has also been suggested that an immense war-weariness had developed in the cities, owing to a lack of food as a consequence of the disruption of agriculture. The feeding of the cities, whose populations were now greatly swollen, was certainly a considerable problem, but the cause of this did not lie in any failure of the harvests, which had not been significantly smaller than in peace-time. The indirect reason was that the government, in order to finance the war, had been printing off millions of rouble notes, and by 1917 inflation had sent prices up to four times what they had been in 1914. The peasantry were consequently faced with the higher cost of purchases, but made no corresponding gain in the sale of their own produce, since this was largely taken by the middlemen on whom they depended. As a result they tended to hoard their grain and to revert to subsistence farming. Thus the cities were constantly short of food; at the same time rising prices led to demands for higher wages in the factories, and in January and February 1916 revolutionary propaganda, aided by German funds, led to widespread strikes (**43, 59**). The outcome of all this, however, was a growing criticism of the government rather than any war-weariness. The original fever of patriotic excitement, which had caused the name of St. Petersburg to be changed to the less German-sounding Petrograd, may have subsided a little in the subsequent years, but it had not turned to defeatism and during the initial risings in Petrograd in February 1917 the crowds in the streets clearly objected to the banners proclaiming 'down with the war'.

The Liberals were now better placed to voice their complaints, since they were participating more fully through a variety of voluntary organizations. Local industrial committees proliferated and in July 1915 a Central War Industries Committee, established under the chairmanship of a prominent Octobrist, Guchkov, included ten workers' representatives – a scheme in which the Petrograd Mensheviks agreed to join despite the objections of their leaders abroad. All this activity gave renewed encouragement to political ambitions and in September 1915 a combination of Kadets and Octobrists in the Duma demanded the forming of a responsible government. Nicholas rejected these proposals. He had by now taken over the position of commander-in-chief of the armed forces and during his absence at his headquarters at Mogilev left most of the day-to-day government in the hands of the Empress who was intensely unpopular, owing to her German origin and the influence that Rasputin, an unsavoury monk, was thought to exercise over her.

All these factors had given rise to a sharp loss of confidence in the regime by 1916. Early in that year, Guchkov had been taking soundings among senior army officers and members of the Central War Industries Committee about a possible coup to force the abdication of the Tsar. In November Milyukov, in a speech in the Duma, openly accused the government of contemplating peace negotiations with Germany. In December a small group of nobles assassinated Rasputin and in January 1917 the Tsar's uncle, Grand Duke Nicholas, was asked indirectly by Prince Lvov whether he would be prepared to take over the throne from his nephew. None of these incidents was in itself the immediate cause of the

February revolution, but they do help to explain why the monarchy survived only a few days after it had broken out.

Meanwhile, the Social Democrat leaders in exile, now mostly in Switzerland, had been the glum spectators of the collapse of international Socialist solidarity. French and German Social Democrats had voted in favour of their respective governments. Plekhanov in Paris had adopted a violently anti-German stand, while Helphand supported the German war effort as the best means of ensuring a revolution in Russia (**69**). The Mensheviks largely maintained that Russia had the right to defend herself against Germany, although Martov, now on the left of his group, demanded an end to the war and a settlement on the basis of national self-determination, with no annexations or indemnities.

It was these views of Martov that predominated in a manifesto drawn up by Trotsky at a conference at Zimmerwald, attended by thirty-five Socialist leaders in September 1915. Inevitably Lenin, supported by Zinoviev and Radek, strongly contested them. Their attitudes became known as the Zimmerwald Left. Lenin rejected both the defence of Russia and the cry for peace. Since the autumn of 1914 he had insisted that 'from the standpoint of the working class and of the labouring masses the lesser evil would be the defeat of the Tsarist monarchy' (**72**); the war must be turned into a civil war of the proletarian soldiers against their own governments, and if a proletarian victory should emerge from this in Russia, then their duty would be to wage a revolutionary war for the liberation of the masses throughout Europe. Thus Lenin remained the *enfant terrible* of the Russian Social Democrat party, although at this point in the war his following in Russia was as little as 10,000 and he must have seemed no more than the leader of an extremist wing of a bankrupt organization.

Part Two: Descriptive Analysis

3 February–October 1917

The Revolution of February 1917 and the Fall of the Monarchy

The revolution that broke out in Petrograd at the end of February 1917 apparently took everyone by surprise. There had been some unrest during the preceding weeks, but this seemed no more than a continuation of the disorders that had harassed the capital in 1916 (see p. 24). On 9 January 150,000 workers in Petrograd came out to commemorate the anniversary of Bloody Sunday of 1905, and the government responded by arresting a few Bolsheviks and the Labour group of the Central War Industries Committee. This was followed by a vast demonstration of 80,000 workers in support of the Duma when it reopened at the Tauride palace on 14 February, and four days later a strike for higher wages began to spread through the Putilov works. None of this, however, was regarded as sufficiently serious by the minister of the interior, Protopopov, to advise the Tsar to remain in Petrograd, and on 22 February Nicholas duly returned by train to his headquarters at Mogilev some 650 kilometres away.

The major upheaval began on the next day, 23 February, when a Socialist celebration of Women's Day brought thousands of women factory workers out on to the streets in the freezing cold. Here they were joined by the Putilov strikers whose management had just declared a lockout and soon the crowds took up a cry for bread, which had been rationed during the past week. In the course of the next two days the number of strikers rose to 240,000 and there were several clashes between mounted police and demonstrators singing the 'Marseillaise' and carrying banners denouncing the autocracy. Yet even now there was little sense of alarm; neither the government nor the Duma paid much attention to this commotion during their deliberations, and General Khabalov, commander of the Petrograd military district, was careful to avoid provocation, forbidding his troops to shoot at the unarmed crowd except in self-defence.

On the whole, there is little evidence that these initial outbreaks were the result of a conspiracy. The left-wing groups were naturally always prepared to make trouble, but their reactions at this time hardly point to any concerted plan of campaign. The celebration of Women's Day had simply happened to coincide with the Putilov strike. The bread shortage may have been exacerbated by recent strikes in the bakeries, where the Bolsheviks were well-established, but it was due principally to the unwillingness of the peasantry to sell their grain to the cities (see p. 24). The only explanation that has been put forward is not really an explanation at all – that the movement was a purely spontaneous one and that it owed little to personal leadership.

Indeed, the events of 26 February suggested that it might soon be all over. On the previous evening General Khabalov had received a telegram from the Tsar at Mogilev: 'I command you to put an end as from tomorrow to all disturbances in the streets. . . .' (**59**). The outcome of this was that rioting in the Znamensky Square on the afternoon of 26 February led to the death of forty demonstrators, when a unit of the Volynsky regiment opened fire on them. Within a few hours, however, there were ominous indications that the troops were unreliable. That evening a mutiny by some soldiers of the Pavlovsky Guards regiment was crushed fairly easily, but on the next day, 27 February, the authorities suddenly lost all command over their military forces when the Volynsky regiment mutinied and the infection spread rapidly to other units. The confusion in the streets had proved too much for the garrison troops who consisted of a miscellaneous collection of young conscripts and soldiers awaiting their return to the front. Sickened by the prospect of firing on unarmed civilians, they began to go over to the crowds, to whom they distributed their weapons, and although the mutiny was certainly not universal, Khabalov, unable to identify the units which were still loyal, was compelled to withdraw to the Winter Palace. By the evening of 27 February Petrograd was in the hands of the insurgents.

At the precise moment of this general breakdown the Duma was faced with a crisis of its own. Early on 27 February Rodzyanko, its president, had received a decree from the premier Golitsyn and the Council of Ministers proroguing it until April. Throughout the day, while chaos reigned in the streets outside, the principal members of the Duma hesitated over defying that order and it was not until the evening that they finally decided to set up a provisional committee which hoped to persuade the Tsar to replace the autocracy with a constitutional monarchy.

This attempt to take over the direction of events was largely prompted by the realization that the Socialist bodies were planning to form a new Petrograd Soviet which might well gain control of the situation. A left-wing member of the Duma, Kerensky, had already told a mass of demonstrators, who had rushed to the Tauride palace, to seize the railway stations, telephone exchanges and post and telegraph offices, and in the afternoon two Menshevik deputies, Chkheidze and Skobelev, had received permission from Rodzyanko to hold a meeting in the Tauride palace. Here that evening a Soviet of some two hundred, which had been rapidly elected by factory workers and soldiers, appointed a provisional executive committee of their own. Thus by the end of the day two committees – one of the Duma and one of the Petrograd Soviet – had each established themselves amid the general hubbub in the Tauride palace. They were of very different political complexion, but they were for the moment united by one common fear – the knowledge that there was little likelihood of an effective resistance if the Tsar attempted to crush the rising with fresh forces from outside Petrograd [**doc. 4**].

At first this appeared to be Nicholas's intention. He ignored all of Rodzyanko's appeals to him by telegraph to consent to a constitutional monarchy, and when on the evening of 27 February he learnt that Khabalov was no longer in control of Petrograd, he sent General Ivanov to the capital to restore order with new troops despatched from the front. On the next day he set off himself from Mogilev for Tsarskoe Selo outside Petrograd, but early on 1 March the news that stations further up the line were in the hands of hostile troops caused the imperial train to proceed instead to Pskov, where the Tsar would be under the protection of General Ruzsky's headquarters on the northern front.

The events of the next two days were governed by the attitudes of the generals (**55, 59**). They had long been uneasy over the manifest incapacity of the Tsar, and Rodzyanko, despairing of making any impact on Nicholas, succeeded in convincing them that the situation in Petrograd could only be contained by the granting of constitutional reforms. At Pskov these views were put by General Ruzsky to the Tsar, who eventually agreed to some grudging concessions. This had the effect of calling off Ivanov's mission, but it was too late to achieve much else. In the early hours of 2 March Rodzyanko informed Ruzsky that the pressure of opinion in Petrograd was now such that the Tsar would have to abdicate if the monarchy was to be saved, and later that day Nicholas decided that if he could not rule as an autocrat, he would rather not rule at all. A few hours later two deputies from the Duma arrived at Pskov to negotiate the final act whereby Nicholas abdicated for himself and his son in favour of his brother, Grand Duke Michael, at the same time appointing Prince Lvov as prime minister. On 3 March, however, Michael, after some consultation, declared that he would not accept the crown unless it was offered to him by a constituent assembly. Thus in this extraordinary way the Romanov monarchy came to an end and the Liberals in the Duma found that they were faced with a republic after all.

The First Provisional Government and the Petrograd Soviet: 2 March–5 May

By 2 March the Duma committee had established a provisional government under Prince Lvov, composed of Octobrists and Kadets, with Milyukov as foreign minister and Guchkov as minister of war and the navy. A series of proclamations announced a complete amnesty for all political and religious offences, full democratic liberties, the end of the death penalty and the confiscation of Crown lands. Meanwhile, the news of the events in Petrograd had spread to the provinces and on 5 March a decree transferred the authority of the former Tsarist governors to the local *zemstvos*, which soon found themselves working somewhat precariously alongside newly-created Soviets.

The crucial assumption of the provisional government was that the war must go on. They needed recognition and support from Russia's western allies, who had been watching the tumult in Petrograd with mixed feelings; the generals, whose continued cooperation was important, naturally shared this view, and so far as public opinion was concerned, there had been no great popular outcry for a separate peace with the Central Powers. This military commitment, however, was constantly to shackle all other aspects of their work. A committee for general land reform had been set up, but it was clear that any major redistribution would play havoc with the army, if the peasant soldiers at the front heard that the estates were being carved up in their absence. Consequently the provisional government, which was in any case nervous of the possibility of social revolution, produced few positive measures, maintaining that all final decisions must await the summoning of a Constituent Assembly. In the minds of many this last represented the great hope for the future, but here again the war created an obstacle in that the presence of millions of soldiers along the front would make the election of such an assembly a lengthy matter and throughout 1917 there was to be constant procrastination.

The odd part of the situation was that while the provisional government was assuming these responsibilities, it could take no effective action without the agreement of the Petrograd Soviet which controlled the railways and the postal and telegraph services. This body had already set up military and food supply commissions and initiated the publication of *Izvestya*. Its most devastating action was the issue of Order No. 1 [**doc. 5**] which made all military orders dependent upon its consent and placed discipline at a regimental level in the hands of soldiers' councils. At first its membership had been drawn purely from the capital, but at the end of March, after local Soviets had sprung up over the entire country, an All-Russian Soviet conference added further delegates in Petrograd and established a central executive committee which claimed to act on behalf of the workers' and soldiers' Soviets, although not the peasantry who were soon to organize a congress of their own.

In these circumstances it is perhaps surprising that the provisional government should have survived at all, since its members had simply been co-opted from a Duma elected on a narrow franchise before the war. The Petrograd Soviet, however, suffered from a lack of confidence that inhibited it from taking over the revolution. Many divisions existed between the various Socialist groups of which it was composed, and the leaders, until recently in exile or in Siberia, were not yet sufficiently in touch with the situation to take an independent line. The Social Revolutionaries were probably the strongest party, but they did not possess a clearly articulated organization, and Chernov, who only returned in April, hoped to play for time by delaying the election of the Constituent Assembly (**91**). The Mensheviks had a more formidable leadership in such figures as Chkheidze, the chairman of the Petrograd Soviet, and Tseretelli and Dan who were prominent members of it, but they were held back by doctrinal considerations. They believed that they were living through a bourgeois revolution, even though it had been brought about initially by the proletariat and the soldiers. Consequently they only aimed at consolidation and their concern with working-class interests was limited for the moment to the establishment of an eight-hour day in the factories.

These hesitant and divided views caused the Soviet to follow a policy of cooperation without actual participation in the provisional government; only Kerensky had a foot in each camp as minister of justice and vice-chairman of the Petrograd Soviet. This compromise meant that the Soviet had to acquiesce in a continuation of the war, although they did stipulate that the eventual peace should be without annexations or indemnities. At first, even the Bolsheviks accepted this general policy for the left. It is true that during the February days the young Molotov had advocated an immediate take-over by the Soviet, but he had been pushed aside by Stalin and Kamenev on their return from Siberia, and the Bolshevik central committee agreed to limited cooperation with the government. Thus the two groups in the Tauride palace were to jog along uneasily together, Prince Lvov's cabinet attempting to govern without power, while the Soviet held the reins of power but would not govern (**23**).

It was not long before the Bolshevik attitude had changed. Bottled up in Switzerland, Lenin had read the news of the February revolution in an agony of frustration. There was no hope of the Allies allowing him to pass through France, but after Helphand in Copenhagen had opened up negotiations with the German authorities, he and a small group of Socialists, including Zinoviev, Radek and Lunacharsky, were allowed to make a remarkable journey through Germany in a sealed train [**doc. 6b**] and on 3 April Lenin eventually arrived at the Finland Station in Petrograd. On the next day he staggered the Social Democrats gathered in the Tauride palace with an utterly uncompromising statement of policy, published later in *Pravda* as the April theses. There must be no cooperation with the provisional government at all. There must be incessant anti-war propaganda; the land must be nationalized and all power go to the Soviets. 'Not a parliamentary republic ... but a republic of Soviets of Workers', Agricultural Labourers' and Peasants' Deputies throughout the whole country from top to bottom.' (**6**). His persuasiveness eventually won his own Bolshevik party round, although only on the understanding that the Soviets should not take over until the Bolsheviks had a majority in them. To all other Socialists, however, Lenin sounded like a madman, and with these demands his party, even now only numbering some 26,000 members, had placed themselves in a state of total isolation.

This divide between Lenin and the other Socialist parties was to grow still more pronounced, when at the end of April a new crisis brought the first provisional government to an end. On 20 April the publication of a diplomatic note by Milyukov had suggested that Russia's war aims were still annexationist, and this was followed by a further outbreak of violence and bloodshed in the streets of Petrograd which only the central executive committee was able eventually to quell. By now the non-Bolshevik members of the Soviet had formed the view that although they were not prepared to take power alone, they could exercise greater control by participating in government, and after some debate with the central executive committee the first coalition was created on 5 May. Prince Lvov remained premier, but ten ministers from the Duma were joined in office by six Socialists, including the Menshevik Tseretelli in charge of communications, Skobelev of labour and the Social Revolutionary Chernov of agriculture, while Kerensky became minister of war.

The Coalition Governments and the Threat from the Left and the Right

The entry into a coalition was a fatal step for the Socialist groups. They had openly assumed a joint responsibility for the actions of a government in which the implementing of their own policies was to be seriously hampered by the presence of the Duma ministers. They were bound to a continuation of the war which the Milyukov note had made highly suspect among many of the left. They were to be associated with the constant delays in the summoning of the Constituent Assembly, and at the ministry of agriculture, Chernov, who wished to press on with the land reforms, was unable to achieve anything against the opposition of the Kadets. Thus, as they drifted on throughout that summer, the coalition Socialists gradually became discredited in the eyes of the masses who saw them increasingly as tools of the conservative classes.

All this suited Lenin well. In the industrial cities a variety of organizations had proliferated at a local level, where they could easily reflect popular discontent. Factory committees supervised appointments and managerial positions; the 976 trade unions representing one and a half million workers in June had grown to more than 2000 representing two and three quarter million by October. Workers' militia groups had been formed and by the autumn there were some 900 Soviets, in which the soldiers in garrison towns often exercised considerable influence (**60**). In the countryside the impatience of the peasantry was leading to a state of anarchy as they began to help themselves to the landowners' estates, and these interpretations of revolution, far more violent that the efforts of the Socialist ministers, were bound to strengthen the Bolshevik party which by August had grown to 200,000. Since Lenin's return the Bolsheviks had had enormously greater financial resources, supplied indirectly by Germany through Helphand [**doc. 6a**]. Their members were active in the provinces, the army and the factories; by June there were forty-one Bolshevik newspapers in circulation, and at the same time Lenin was creating his own striking force of Red Guards – workers armed with rifles – who by July numbered some 10,000 in the Petrograd factories.

At the same time the divisions among his Socialist opponents were becoming more pronounced. Martov, who had returned to Russia in May, was on the extreme left of the Mensheviks in opposition to the war and the coalition (**75**). A left faction of the Social Revolutionaries took the same view, particularly when it became known that Kerensky was preparing a new summer offensive; and a Social Revolutionary conference in August, at which they gained one-third of the seats, suggested that the party was seriously split. Lenin, however, made no move to ally with these dissentients. He was simply content to outbid all the other parties, as, for example, at a congress of Soviets of peasants' deputies in May when he openly encouraged the peasantry to commandeer the estates.

Nevertheless, the new sense of extremism was to take a little time to percolate through the electoral processes. When the first All-Russian congress of Soviets of workers' and soldiers' deputies met on 3 June, the Bolshevik delegates numbered 105, but although this pointed to a marked growth, they were flanked by 248 Mensheviks and 285 Social Revolutionaries, and the new central executive committee of some 250, which it appointed, was drawn largely from these two groups and was to remain as the permanent representative body until the second congress in October. In fact, the attitudes at work in Petrograd were considerably more radical than those of the congress and this was well illustrated on 18 June, when the congress organized a demonstration in general support of the revolution and then found that the vast majority of banners were inscribed with Bolshevik slogans.

This sense of disillusionment which the rank and file felt over the leadership of the left came to a head on 3 July, when factory workers, soldiers and sailors from the nearby island naval base of Kronstadt marched on the Tauride Palace and demanded that the Soviets should take power.

Descriptive Analysis

This has sometimes been regarded by the right as Lenin's first attempt to seize power. In fact, it would seem unlikely. Lenin himself was away at the time, taking a short rest in Finland. Views in the Bolshevik central committee were divided, and although on 4 July they demanded that the demonstrations should continue, this was probably only because they dared not disappoint the participants, whose support they would need later. On the whole, they remained extremely hesitant throughout the affair, and Trotsky, who had returned from New York in May and was now close to the moment when he would join the Bolsheviks, personally intervened to save Chernov from being lynched by the crowd (**80**). At the most, it was probably a local explosion of discontent, heightened by the news of the failure of the offensive which Kerensky had launched against the Central Powers a fortnight before (**64, 89**).

Certainly the episode did Lenin little good. The central executive committee would not budge. The most that they would do was to reject a proposal outlawing the Bolshevik party, who had naturally got the blame for the outbreak, and the government called in forces from the front to quell the disorders which lasted some three days. Prince Lvov resigned and on 24 July Kerensky became head of the second coalition government which took advantage of the situation to denounce the Bolshevik leaders as traitors in German pay. Lenin and Zinoviev went into hiding; Kamenev and others were arrested; so, too, a fortnight later were Trotsky and Lunacharsky, after Trotsky had finally decided to throw in his lot with the Bolsheviks and characteristically wrote a letter to the government to that effect.

These measures were not so rigorous as to prevent the meeting of a Bolshevik party congress shortly afterwards, but Kerensky clearly reckoned that the threat from that quarter had been silenced for the moment and now set out to consolidate his position with the other parties. In the middle of August he summoned a state conference at Moscow, but since the propertied classes were fairly strongly represented and the Bolsheviks predictably declared a boycott, the occasion only served to demonstrate the continuing gulf between the extremes.

The real tragedy for Kerensky was that immediately after he had put down the movement from the left, he was faced with what appeared to him to be an attempt at a counter-revolutionary coup from the right. On taking office, he had appointed General Kornilov as commander-in-chief and had tried to strengthen his hand by restoring the death penalty at the front, a move which had been accepted by the central executive committee. Kornilov, however, together with several other general officers, believed that there could be no checking the gradual drift towards chaos, unless discipline in the army were totally restored, and the German capture of Riga on 21 August added to the sense of urgency. Kornilov wanted an extension of the death penalty behind the lines, the establishment of military control over forms of supply and the removal of political agitators and soldiers' councils. To a Socialist this suggested the classic pattern of a military counter-revolution with Kornilov in the role of Bonaparte, and although Kerensky recognized the need to strengthen his government, he knew that such proposals would certainly be resisted by the Petrograd Soviet.

As a consequence, there had been some discussion over the dispatch of the Third Cavalry Corps to Petrograd to deal with the Soviet when the new measures were announced, and on 22 August Kornilov, in conversation with Savinkov, the deputy minister of war, certainly seems to have thought that he had the government's agreement on this (**87**). Naturally, the position was a delicate one for Kerensky as a spokesman of the left, and eventually his vacillation had hardened into a conviction that Kornilov was planning a right-wing coup. Accordingly, on the evening of 26 August, Kerensky dismissed him and demanded additional powers for himself from his council of ministers, at which three Kadet ministers resigned. Kornilov now issued a manifesto denouncing the Bolsheviks in the Soviets and demanding continued resistance to Germany and the summoning of a constituent assembly, and began an advance on Petrograd.

Inevitably Kerensky was thrust back to reliance on the left who at once closed their ranks. A council set up by the central executive committee to defend Petrograd included Bolshevik representatives whose leaders were released from prison; arms were distributed to a workers' militia, a move which enabled the Bolsheviks to strengthen their own Red Guards, repressed in the aftermath of the July days. Local committees in the towns on Kornilov's route were to deprive him of the use of railways and telegraph services, and agitators were sent out to undermine the loyalty of his troops, who indeed had little idea of what was happening. In the event this last proved decisive; there was virtually no fighting, since Kornilov's forces simply melted away, and by 2 September Kornilov himself had been taken prisoner.

Nevertheless, the whole episode spelt disaster for Kerensky. The excitement of making a stand against a counter-revolutionary attack broke down any remaining restraints. Discipline in the Russian army had been disintegrating throughout the summer under the influence of Order No. 1, greatly exploited by Bolshevik agents, and now it finally collapsed; officers were murdered and there were wholesale desertions as peasant soldiers streamed back to their villages. In the provinces the take-over of estates accelerated and the attempts by Kerensky to check this with punitive Cossack expeditions only increased the sense of antagonism. In the cities a continuing inflation had by now reduced the value of the rouble to one-tenth of what it had been in 1914, and this had strengthened demands for shorter hours and higher wages. In the ensuing strikes and lock-outs the factory committees had by the autumn gained almost complete control and at an All-Russian conference of factory committees meeting at Petrograd more than 50 per cent of the voting delegates were Bolshevik. Among the workers' militia groups – with a membership of more than 15,000 in Petrograd – sympathy seemed to be shifting towards Lenin's own Red Guards, and it was not surprising that in the Soviets, whose deputies were constantly subject to recall by their electors, the Bolsheviks should make considerable gains. On 31 August they achieved a majority in the Petrograd Soviet; on 5 September they won the Moscow Soviet of workers' deputies, and throughout Russia major industrial centres appeared to be going the same way.

Against this background of growing anarchy, in which, as Lenin said, the masses were becoming more Bolshevik than the Bolsheviks themselves, Kerensky struggled to find some central position on which he could base a government. For this he summoned a Democratic Conference which opened at Petrograd on 14 September. The propertied classes were excluded, but the representation of the various Socialist bodies was so arranged as to leave the Bolsheviks in a minority. The Bolshevik delegation only attended long enough to walk out after a mocking denunciation by Trotsky, who on 23 September was elected chairman of the Petrograd Soviet. Even after their departure, however, the conference still failed to give Kerensky a mandate to include Kadet ministers in a reorganized coalition, since the left now saw them as the allies of Kornilov.

On this Kerensky went ahead on his own, took four Kadets into a new government and set up a pre-Parliament to act as a consultative body until the meeting of the Constituent Assembly, for which elections were at last to take place in November. The members of the pre-Parliament, which opened its first session on 7 October in the Marinsky Palace, were drawn partly from the Democratic Conference, but also from the propertied classes and the non-Socialist parties. Once again the Bolsheviks withdrew, after Trotsky had delivered another tirade against the government, which was now suspected of intending to abandon Petrograd to the German army, and Kerensky was left with a nominated cabinet of ministers that made little appeal to the right or the left.

4 The Bolshevik Seizure of Power: October 1917

Since the beginning of September Lenin had been convinced that the time was ripe for the party to take power by force, and from his various hiding places in Finland he had been bombarding the Bolshevik central committee with demands for action. His sense of urgency was heightened by the fear that the favourable moment could easily pass; with further delay the masses in their impatience might begin to lose faith in the Bolsheviks; equally, there was always the danger of a fresh counter-revolutionary attack from the right.

To his colleagues on the Bolshevik central committee at their headquarters in the Smolny Institute at Petrograd this policy sounded highly adventurous. With the tide of opinion moving so strongly in their direction it would surely be safer to await the second All-Russian congress of Soviets, which was due to meet that autumn, rather than to run the risk of a local insurrection. There was, too, that fundamental obstacle which had already inhibited the Mensheviks in the course of 1917 and which also worried some of the Bolsheviks. Russia at the present stage of her development was not ready for the proletarian revolution and to attempt to carry it through now would be premature, hence disastrous. In answer to this Lenin argued passionately that he was not contemplating insurrection in Russia alone. He believed that the whole of Europe, particularly Germany, was on the verge of a genuinely proletarian rising, and a Bolshevik seizure of power in Russia would provide the spark for the creation of a Socialist Europe within which a Russian revolution could perfectly well survive.

It is hard to know whether Lenin would ever have got his way in his absence, but on 10 October he came secretly to Petrograd to put the matter beyond doubt at a meeting of twelve members of the committee. The main opposition came from Zinoviev and Kamenev who maintained that an insurrection would be crushed; furthermore, even if it were successful, they saw little indication of revolution in the rest of Europe and therefore no justification for attempting to establish a dictatorship of the proletariat in Russia, still just at the beginning of the bourgeois stage in the Marxist sequence. It was only after hours of argument that Lenin was able to drive the rest of them round to his point of view, and the proposal to take power was eventually carried by ten votes to two – perhaps the most momentous decision of the twentieth century. In the struggle Lenin had had an ally in Trotsky, but their attitudes were not absolutely identical. Trotsky wished to postpone the insurrection until the eve of the second All-Russian congress of Soviets, which could then be presented with a *fait accompli*; Lenin wanted the Red Guards to attack straight away, not necessarily beginning in Petrograd, since he suspected that in their fear of a Bolshevik majority the Mensheviks and Social Revolutionaries on the central executive committee would delay the summoning of the congress as long as possible.

The decision taken on the night of 10 October [**doc. 8**] was confirmed at a larger meeting six days later, but because Lenin was still in hiding he could not exercise control over the detail of the operation which ultimately worked in accordance with Trotsky's timing. On 12 October the executive committee of the Petrograd Soviet had set up a military revolutionary committee for the purpose of supervising the defence of the capital, in case the government should proceed with any plans for abandoning it to the Germans. Predominantly Bolshevik in membership and under the control of Trotsky in his capacity as chairman of the Soviet, this provided an excellent screen for the immediate preparations. By 21 October the regimental committees of the Petrograd garrison had accepted the military revolutionary committee as their supreme authority; thousands of rifles were distributed to the Red Guards, and on 23 October the troops in the Peter-Paul fortress whose allegiance had until then been an unknown quantity were won over by a visit from Trotsky, a move which put a further 100,000 rifles at the Bolsheviks' disposal.

It was not until 24 October that Kerensky began to react. That morning he closed the editorial offices of two Bolshevik newspapers and ordered the cruiser *Aurora*, dangerously close to the Winter Palace, to put to sea. By now, however, it had been settled that the second All-Russian congress of Soviets would meet on the evening of the following day and Trotsky decided that the time had come to commence hostilities. The editorial offices were re-opened, the orders to the *Aurora* were countermanded by the military revolutionary committee, and the Smolny Institute was hastily fortified against attack. In the afternoon Kerensky addressed the pre-

Parliament in the hope of mustering support, but found that he had lost the confidence of Mensheviks and Social Revolutionaries who backed Martov's motion for peace negotiations and an immediate settlement of the land question as the only means of forestalling the Bolsheviks. That evening Trotsky gave the final orders for the coup, and Lenin, arriving in disguise at Smolny, found to his relief that the insurrection was already under way.

Throughout the night detachments of Red Guards and soldiers took possession of the key positions – stations, telephone exchanges, post offices, the national bank and the Tauride Palace. These forces were not particularly disciplined, but like Khabalov the previous February Kerensky found that he had nothing to put against them and on the morning of 25 October he escaped by car from Petrograd to raise troops from the front, while the rest of his government assembled in the Winter Palace. In the afternoon the pre-Parliament was forcibly dispersed by Red Guards, and Lenin and Trotsky declared to the Petrograd Soviet that a new Soviet government would be formed. In fact, Kerensky's government was still nominally in existence, since the assault on the Winter Palace had been delayed to await the arrival of sailors from Kronstadt and it was not until late that night that a half-hearted defence by some officer cadets and a women's battalion was overcome, the palace occupied and the ministers placed under arrest.

Meanwhile, as that attack went on, the second All-Russian congress of Soviets was assembling at Smolny. This was a very different type of body from the first congress which had met in June. The new mood in Russia had produced a majority for the Bolsheviks who, out of a total of 650 seats, held 390 against 80 Mensheviks and about 180 Social Revolutionaries – Left and Right – and it was obvious that the congress would give Lenin everything that he wanted. Amid noisy excitement in a hall thick with cigarette smoke the retiring central executive committee was replaced by a prae-sidium, largely Bolshevik, and Kamenev took the chair (**22**). Against the distant thunder of the *Aurora*, still bombarding the Winter Palace with blank shot, the leaders of the Menshevik groups and the Right Social Revolutionaries uttered their protests, demanding that the fighting should stop and that a left-wing coalition be formed, but their only weapon was to threaten to withdraw from the Congress. This in effect simply strengthened the Bolshevik position, and at the same time confirmed the split in the Social Revolutionary Party, whose left wing decided to stay. 'You are miserable isolated individuals,' cried Trotsky, as Martov and his section of Mensheviks left the hall. 'You are bankrupt. You have played out your role. Go where you belong: to the dust heap of history' (**80**). Then in the early hours of the morning the news of the capture of the Winter Palace arrived at last, and the congress proclaimed that the Soviets had now assumed power throughout Russia.

Lenin himself did not appear until the second session which opened on the following evening of 26 October. An American eye-witness, John Reed, described the scene: 'Now Lenin, gripping the edge of the reading stand, letting his little winking eyes travel over the crowd as he stood there waiting, apparently oblivious to the long rolling ovation which lasted several minutes. When it finished, he said simply, "We shall now proceed to construct the Socialist order!" Again that overwhelming human roar' (**22**). First, there came the peace decree; there was to be an end to secret diplomacy and negotiations would begin at once for a general peace with the Central Powers without annexations or indemnities. Second, the land decree confiscated without compensation all estates previously owned by landlords and the Church. The final arrangements for the redistribution would be settled by the Constituent Assembly, but as a guiding principle every peasant family was to have as much land as they could till without the use of hired labour. As Lenin commented sardonically in his speech, the Bolsheviks had simply taken over the main points of the Social Revolutionaries' programme and he was careful not to lay down any ultimate policy of nationalization. The last item was the selection of a government consisting of a council of heads of departments. Trotsky had already suggested privately that these should be known as commissars to avoid the bourgeois title of 'minister'. 'The Council of Peoples' Commissars?' said Lenin. 'That's splendid; smells terribly of revolution' (**24**). This was to be no coalition; the membership was entirely Bolshevik with Lenin as chairman and including Trotsky for foreign affairs and Stalin for nationalities, and the nominations, like the two decrees, were carried with immense enthusiasm. The congress finally came to a close at five in the morning on 27 October after the election of a new central executive committee in which two thirds of the places went to the Bolsheviks.

Meanwhile Kerensky, frantically searching for troops, was finding that after the Kornilov affair the generals had no further faith in him. The commander of the northern front, Cheremisov, countermanded his orders for troops to advance on Petrograd and his only support came from General Krasnov who offered 700

41

Cossacks and the promise of reinforcements from elsewhere in the line. The Cossacks at least advanced through Gatchina, reaching Tsarskoe Selo on 28 October. On the next day officer cadets attempted an uprising in Petrograd which the Bolsheviks were able to crush, while Krasnov, only a few kilometres away, made no move, awaiting reinforcements that never came. Finally on the night of 30 October a large but highly unorganized Red force [**doc. 9**] repulsed a Cossack attack on the Pulkovo heights (see map p. 50) just outside Petrograd; a few days later Krasnov's forces disintegrated under the pressure of Bolshevik propaganda and Kerensky had to make his escape from Russia. The struggle for Moscow lasted longer, only ending on 2 November after the Bolsheviks had shelled the Kremlin, by which time many of the larger industrial cities had recognized the new Soviet power. Exhausted but triumphant, the Bolshevik leaders could reckon that for the moment their gamble had succeeded. The question now was how long they could survive.

5 The Bolshevik Retention of Power

Any immediate military threat to the Bolsheviks ended with the defeat of Kerensky at Pulkovo. It was to take some time for the conservative interests – the Whites – to muster their forces, and during the next few months the principal resistance to Lenin came from the Socialist organizations in Petrograd. The struggle went on simultaneously over a number of issues (**66**). First, there was the continuing demand that the Bolsheviks should share their power in a broad left-wing coalition. Second, there were objections to aspects of Lenin's plans for the future management of land and industry. Third, the harshness of the terms of the treaty of Brest-Litovsk imposed on Russia by Germany in March 1918 caused a large section of the left to clamour for a renewal of the war. All this created serious division within the Bolshevik central committee itself, and the conflict with the other Socialist groups grew so violent that by the summer of 1918 the government was depending increasingly on a policy of terror.

The Demand for a Socialist Coalition

The situation that confronted the Council of People's Commissars (*Sovnarkom*) in the days following the Bolshevik coup was certainly daunting. None of them had had any previous experience of government and they had now to cope with the state of anarchy which had helped to bring them to power. The civil servants in their departments were on strike and the officials of the State bank were refusing to release any funds. The only areas of Russia where they could be sure of exercising control were in the vicinity of Petrograd and Moscow and in some of the large industrial centres; in many cities the Bolsheviks still had to work in conjunction with other left-wing groups in local Soviets and committees of public safety, and in Petrograd itself the shortage of food was so great that the commissars themselves had to be content with a diet of black bread and vegetable soup. Soldiers, sailors and industrial workers might respond to appeals, but they were in no mood to take orders, particularly after the looting of wine shops and the cellars of the Winter Palace had turned the capital into a scene of drunken orgy (**80**).

None of this deflected Lenin from his determination that the Bolsheviks should rule alone. The resistance which he could expect to this varied. The Mensheviks, whose two factions under Dan and Martov did not reunite until May 1918, could rely on little more than moral pleas. Others, however, were more dangerous. The Social Revolutionaries under Chernov still had considerable support from the peasantry, and the leaders of the railwaymen's union declared that they would withhold the use of the railways from the government, if no left-wing coalition was formed – thus making it impossible to send reinforcements to Moscow where fighting was still going on.

Most serious of all, the dispute was also reflected in the Bolshevik central committee. Kamenev and others were convinced that the Bolsheviks could not manage on their own and tentative negotiations were opened with the other groups, who insisted on the disarming of the Bolshevik detachments and the exclusion of Lenin and Trotsky from any future government. Lenin, who had initially regarded the negotiations as a means of playing for time, naturally saw such talk as treason and was prepared to bring the divide out into the open. 'If you wish a split, go ahead,' he said. 'If you get a majority, take the power in the central executive committee and carry on. We shall go to the sailors' (**1**). At the same time the dispute was exacerbated by the government's control of the press, to which some moderate Bolsheviks objected, and when on 4 November the central executive committee supported Lenin over the suppression of bourgeois newspapers, five members of the Bolshevik central committee resigned – Kamenev, Rykov, Milyutin, Zinoviev and Nogin, three of whom were commissars.

For the moment the most pressing problem was the attitude of the Social Revolutionaries, strongly represented in a congress of peasants' deputies which opened in Petrograd on 11 November. The split in their party, however, had finally been confirmed on the night of 25 October when the Left Social Revolutionaries had sided with the Bolsheviks, and the congress soon broke up into two separate gatherings. This was a relatively easy situation for Lenin to exploit. The Right Social Revolutionaries' assembly was virtually suppressed by being deprived of its rations, while a deal with the Left allowed them to enter the government on the Bolsheviks' terms. Three of them became commissars in *Sovnarkom*, and 108 peasant delegates were added to the central executive committee as well as a further 100 from the army and the navy and 50 from the trade unions (**66**).

With this compromise it seemed that Lenin had gone a long way towards retaining a Bolshevik predominance. The railwaymen's union declared themselves satisfied with the new situation and other strikes were overcome when the authority of the trade union leaders was undermined by a direct approach to their rank and file. The revolt within the Bolshevik party, too, died away. There had been no leaders among them who could seriously challenge Lenin and under threat of expulsion they soon made their peace with the party. Zinoviev, who had recanted almost at once, was reinstated in the central committee, and the other four were readmitted a little later. Meanwhile, in the Soviets in the provincial cities, where Bolsheviks were still having to share power, commissars from the capital proceeded to set up congresses of Soviets, which claimed to have a higher authority and were largely Bolshevik in composition. They were also aided in their efforts by the practice of Social Revolutionaries and Mensheviks to withdraw in protest at the use of force in the Soviets, as they had done from the second All-Russian congress of Soviets at Smolny in October 1917, and this naturally left the field to the Bolsheviks (**60**).

There still remained one further difficulty – the long awaited Constituent Assembly. Amid the revolutionary fervour of 1917 this had acquired the aura of a sovereign body which would finally devise the future form of Russian government. Its election was due to take place on 12 November in accordance with the arrangements already made by Kerensky; the franchise was to be far wider than that for the All-Russian congress of Soviets of workers' and soldiers' deputies, and with the strong support that the Social Revolutionaries enjoyed among the peasantry there seemed little likelihood of a Bolshevik majority. Postponement, however, was out of the question in view of public opinion, and Lenin fell back on influencing its composition after the polling by arresting the leading Kadets and by trying to persuade electors to revise the lists of delegates whom they had returned. None of this had much effect. Out of 715 seats the Bolsheviks gained 175 with a popular vote of about nine million; the Left Social Revolutionaries had only 40 seats, the Kadets and the Mensheviks still less, and they were all utterly outnumbered by the Right Social Revolutionaries who won 370 seats with a popular vote of twenty-one million.

To the Bolsheviks, faced with this inconvenient outcome of a reasonably democratic election, it was clear that the Constituent Assembly could not be allowed to survive. On the first day of its meeting in the Tauride Palace – 5 January 1918 – Sverdlov read out a statement from the central executive committee that the Assembly must regard itself as subservient to the congress of Soviets and the decrees of *Sovnarkom*. When this was rejected by 237 to 138 votes, the Bolsheviks and the Left Social Revolutionaries withdrew. Debate continued until four o'clock in the morning, when the commander of the guard announced that the session would now close 'because the guard is tired', and later that day Lenin formally dissolved the Assembly on the grounds that the Left Social Revolutionaries were inadequately represented. The only protest was a march by the Social Revolutionaries through Petrograd, but since Chernov had insisted that they should be unarmed and that there should be no appeal to some army units who were known to be sympathetic, they were easily dispersed by the Red Guards. In this way the Constituent Assembly, of which so much had been expected, came to a speedy end and a few days later a third All-Russian congress of Soviets, whose election was rather more under Bolshevik control, gave their formal approval of Lenin's action.

Disagreements over Social and Economic Policy

'It was impossible to tell in advance,' wrote Trotsky many years later, 'whether we were to stay in power or be overthrown . . .' (**24**) and in those first precarious weeks Lenin lost no time in defining the practical features of the new Bolshevik order. A flood of decrees issued from *Sovnarkom* which met for six hours every day under his chairmanship at the Smolny Institute. The separation of church and state was proclaimed; marriage was to be a civil ceremony and divorce could be had virtually on demand. Municipal authorities were made responsible for all food, and shops and restaurants were brought under their control. On 14 December the resistance of the banks was overcome with a military occupation; the central executive committee declared banking to be a state monopoly and on 21 January 1918 all Tsarist domestic and foreign debts were annulled. The landed classes had already seen their estates taken over by the peasantry and now the bourgeois were to suffer a similar fate. The personal ownership of large houses was declared illegal, and on 29 December 1917 dividends ceased to be paid and share dealings were prohibited. Local Soviets, taking their lead from Smolny, forced wealthy residents to hand over large sums of money under the threat of imprisonment or of forced labour in the mines, and what remained of private capital was soon to be destroyed in a wild inflation as the government printed off millions of rouble notes.

It was not only the dispossessed who deplored the early activities of the Bolsheviks. The left-wing groups too were disturbed and puzzled over the attitude that Lenin adopted towards land and industry. Doctrinally the Bolsheviks had stood for the end of private ownership. On the land this should have meant setting up a system of state collective farms. The peasantry, however, were clearly determined to act on the Social Revolutionaries' programme for a division of the land into millions of tiny holdings and, as has been seen, Lenin had already accepted this position with the land decree of 26 October. For him this was a purely tactical manoeuvre; eventually he hoped to find a new revolutionary force among the poorer peasants who could be turned against the richer ones, but for the moment he was certain that there could be no rapid reversion to the original Bolshevik plan of collectivization.

The implementing of his land policy caused difficulty on two fronts. Within the Bolshevik party a more doctrinaire group, known as the Left Communists, led by Bukharin, Radek and Smirnov, considered Lenin's manoeuvre heretical in that it would lead to the growth of a large class of capitalist farmers who could become an insuperable obstacle to the creation of a Socialist society. Outside the party the Social Revolutionaries could feel more satisfied. The land committees, where their influence predominated, were sometimes overruled by the local Soviets, but in the main the partitioning of the estates went as they wanted – with the richer peasant doing best of all [**doc. 14**]. There were, nevertheless, other factors that aroused their suspicions. They resented the Bolsheviks' forcible requisitioning of grain from the peasantry, a policy dictated by the failure of food supply which had brought the major cities close to starvation (see p. 60). There was, too, an ominous note in the law for the socialization of land, promulgated in February 1918, which recognized individual farming but also spoke of eventually developing 'the collective system of agriculture as being more economic in respect both of labour and of products, at the expense of individual holdings, in order to bring about the transition to a Socialist economy' (**53**).

In industry circumstances were to drive Lenin to a different type of compromise. Before assuming power the Bolsheviks had not imagined any incompatibility between nationalization and workers' control. Factory committees would take over the management of production, all within a general framework laid down by the central executive committee of the Soviets. The trouble was that the workers, like the peasantry, were more interested in becoming their own masters, and the ousting of proprietors and managers, which had continued throughout 1917, suggested an anarchy of individual factories each run by its own committee.

At the time workers' control had been too powerful a force to resist and in any case, until the October coup, the Bolsheviks were content to see this as a means of undermining the successive provisional governments. Once in power, however, Lenin was convinced that workers' control must be subordinated to the requirements of state capitalism, if the Bolshevik regime was to survive. Two developments followed from this. First, the sheer incompetence of the factory committees caused Lenin to advocate control under a single director rather than an elected committee, and former managers and technical specialists were reinstated, often on high salaries [**doc. 12a**]. Second, the Supreme Council of National Economy (*Vesenkha*) was established on 2 December in order to create a general state control through its local organs (*Glavki*) although in the early days its practical authority was small (**85**).

Both these aspects of Lenin's industrial policy were anathema to the Left Social Revolutionaries and to the Left Communists alike. They deplored the negotiations with capitalist owners, the use of non-Communist specialists and the undermining of workers' control. The Left Social Revolutionaries, with their Populist ante-cedents, disliked the whole idea of the state; the Left Communists expected it to wither away, now that the proletarian revolution had been accomplished, and they predicted that Lenin's encouragement of state capitalism would lead to a bureaucratic centralization in which the rule of commissars would soon destroy the independence of the local Soviets [**doc. 12b**]. And in May 1918 Lenin seemed to justify these fears, when in his *Left Infantilism and the petty bourgeois spirit* he advised Russian Socialists 'to study the state capitalism of the Germans, to adopt it with all possible strength, not to spare dictatorial methods in order to hasten its adoption . . ' (**53**).

The Treaty of Brest-Litovsk: March 1918

It was the issue of peace with the Central Powers that was to lead to the most violent debate of all. A cease-fire had been ordered a fortnight after the Bolshevik coup, and during the next two months a series of meetings took place between the two sides at the fortress of Brest-Litovsk just behind the German lines. For the Central Powers the negotiations were principally in the hands of General Hoffmann and the German foreign minister Baron von Kühlmann, while the Bolshevik delegation was headed first by Adolf Joffe and then after 22 December by Trotsky (**95**).

Throughout the proceedings the Bolsheviks were torn between two conflicting considerations – the need to produce the rapid peace which they had promised, and the desire to play for time while awaiting the revolution in central Europe on which they had based their hopes. Initially they aimed at a general peace including the entente Powers, and insisted furthermore that it should be without annexations by either side. On this last they had even declared that they would grant independence to the western borderlands of the former Russian empire – Finland, the Baltic provinces, Poland and the Ukraine – although their ultimate purpose was to establish Soviet republics in these new states.

None of this seemed likely to be fulfilled. The entente Powers had made it clear by the end of 1917 that they would carry on with the war, even if Russia dropped out. Over annexations, the principal issue at Brest-Litovsk, the Germans refused to give up the territory of Lithuania, Courland and Poland which they already occupied, since they had a clear idea of Bolshevik intentions there. The Bolsheviks suspected equally correctly that the Germans proposed to turn these areas into puppet states of their own, and the arrival of a Ukrainian nationalist delegation at Brest-Litovsk suggested that they were prepared to use local separatism to deprive Russia of still more territory. The Ukraine was of particular significance for Austria-Hungary who, faced with hunger riots in Vienna, hoped desperately to be able to draw on its food-producing regions. It was also a weak spot for the Russian government. In the summer of 1917 Ukrainian nationalists had proclaimed an autonomous republic, but after the election of an Assembly – the *Rada* – had shown that the Bolsheviks had only limited support, relations between Petrograd and Kiev had gradually broken down, until by the end of the year the Ukrainian Bolsheviks had withdrawn to create a rival base at Kharkov where they summoned an All-Ukrainian congress of Soviets.

Trotsky returned to Petrograd for further consultation on 7 January 1918, just after the Constituent Assembly had been dispersed, and found that by now Lenin was convinced that the

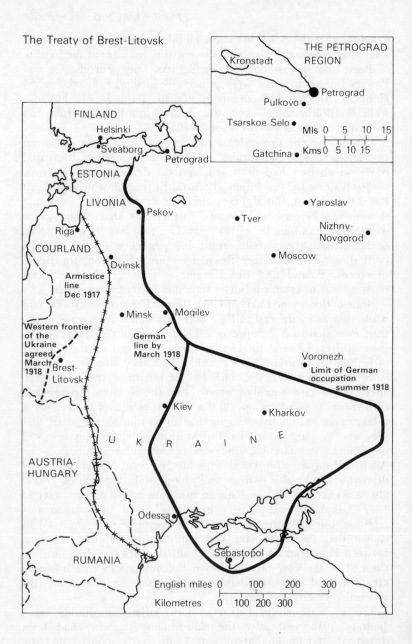

The Treaty of Brest-Litovsk

THE PETROGRAD REGION

Kronstadt

Petrograd

Pulkovo

Tsarskoe Selo

Mls 0 5 10 15

Gatchina

Kms 0 5 10 15

FINLAND

Helsinki

Sveaborg

Petrograd

ESTONIA

LIVONIA

Pskov

Yaroslav

Tver

Riga

Nizhny-Novgorod

COURLAND

Dvinsk

Moscow

Armistice
line
Dec 1917

Minsk

Mogilev

Western frontier
of the
Ukraine
agreed
March
1918

German
line by
March 1918

Brest-Litovsk

Voronezh

Limit of German
occupation
summer 1918

Kiev

Kharkov

U K R A I N E

AUSTRIA-
HUNGARY

Odessa

Sebastopol

RUMANIA

English miles 0   100   200   300

Kilometres 0   100 200 300

German terms must be accepted. This view was opposed by the Left Communists under Bukharin who declared that hostilities should be renewed, and from an informal vote among leading Bolsheviks on 8 January it seemed that there was a considerable majority in favour of rejecting the terms. Three days later, however, Lenin did manage to persuade the Bolshevik central committee to postpone any final decision, but only by taking refuge in a curious formula put forward by Trotsky – no war, no peace – whereby Russia would withdraw from the war without signing any peace with Germany.

On 17 January Trotsky resumed the negotiations at Brest-Litovsk. This time he was accompanied by three representatives of the Ukrainian Soviet and was encouraged by the knowledge that Russian forces were at that moment assisting Ukrainian Bolsheviks in crushing the *Rada* government at Kiev. The Germans, however, ignored this and on 27 January signed a treaty with the Ukrainian nationalist delegation, whereby certain western border districts of the Ukraine were to be included within Austria-Hungary and a million tons of foodstuffs were to be put at the disposal of the Central Powers. Two days later Trotsky flung down his unconventional formula to the shocked astonishment of General Hoffmann and returned to Petrograd.

No war, no peace was soon shown to be an empty gesture. On 18 February* the Germans began an unopposed advance through Estonia and after the arrival of the news that Dvinsk had fallen an anguished debate in the Bolshevik central committee gave Lenin a majority of one in favour of reopening negotiations. The Germans took four days to reply and then put up their terms. The frontier was to be shifted further east and all Russian forces were to be withdrawn from Livonia, Estonia, Finland and the Ukraine – a surrender of most of Russia's western territories including 34 per cent of her population, 32 per cent of her agricultural land and 54 per cent of her industrial concerns.

This would be a truly crippling blow for Russia and it was small wonder that Bukharin and his war party should return to the attack. They could not accept the loss of the rich agricultural regions of the Ukraine, which, they argued, would also become a centre of counter-revolution. In the spirit of the Zimmerwald Left

---

* At the end of January 1918 the Bolshevik government brought the Russian calendar into line with the rest of Europe. This leap of thirteen days means that 18 February was only a week after Trotsky had left Brest-Litovsk.

they demanded the opening of a revolutionary war whose emotional appeal would enable Russia to create a new army out of the ruin of the old at a time when Germany's military commitment in the west would prevent her from making any major offensive eastwards.

Against this Lenin posed a hard-headed realism. He declared that it was vital that Bolshevik Russia should gain a breathing space. He knew that the Russian army was in no state to confront the German military machine; Trotsky himself had seen that the Russian trenches were virtually empty of soldiers when he had crossed the front line on the way to Brest-Litovsk. In any case, reports in December had suggested that the only reliable Russian forces were anti-Bolshevik and this might offer an opportunity for their left-wing opponents to weaken the Bolshevik hold; and tentative enquiries had revealed that there was little likelihood of support from the west in the event of a renewal of hostilities. The fundamental factor in Lenin's mind was that he had by now despaired of any immediate revolution breaking out in central Europe [**doc. 11**] – an interesting vindication of the objections raised by Zinoviev and Kamenev the previous October.

In the end, after a long struggle with the Bolshevik central committee, Lenin did get his way. It was, however, only his threat of resignation and Trotsky's support that enabled him to carry a vote of seven in favour of peace against four abstentions and four in favour of war (**80**). Bukharin, Uritsky, Bubnov and Lomov now in their turn threatened to resign from office, but all except Bukharin were eventually persuaded to remain. On 3 March a small Russian delegation signed the treaty of Brest-Litovsk. At the same time the German army proceeded to overrun the Ukraine, where both the local Soviet and the *Rada* government were suppressed and a puppet administration was set up under Hetman Skoropadsky. The Germans had stipulated that ratification must follow within two weeks and this duly took place on 16 March, but not in Petrograd. Lenin had reckoned that the German army and the frontiers of an independent Finland were now too dangerously close to the Russian capital, and accordingly, on 10 March, he shifted the seat of government to Moscow, where the fourth All-Russian congress of Soviets meeting in the Kremlin finally ratified the peace by 784 votes to 261.

The Growth of Terror

All these tensions among the left-wing groups were not eased by the realization that the methods used by the Bolsheviks were likely to reinforce their monopoly of power. The proposals to control the press had already created alarm and at the same time there were clear signs that the Bolsheviks were turning to a policy of terror – as their critics had always predicted. In December 1917 a secret decree established a special section of the military revolutionary committee as the Cheka, a commission of eight under Dzerzhinsky, which was to make war on 'counter-revolution and sabotage'. 'Until we apply terror – shooting on the spot – to speculators,' said Lenin early in 1918, 'we shall achieve nothing' (**53**), and the Cheka which at first was content to confiscate ration books soon resorted to summary executions – 6,300 in that year according to the official figure, although this was almost certainly an underestimate [**doc. 10**]. The crimes of the victims were often no more than their social class or their political views [**doc. 13**], and among the left-wing groups moral abhorrence soon grew into personal apprehensiveness. Ironically the death penalty, abolished in October 1917, was not formally restored until June 1918, when there was an outburst of protest at the recent shootings. 'Human life became cheaper,' wrote Martov, 'cheaper than the paper on which the executioner writes the order for its destruction . . .' (**75**).

Indeed, it seemed only too likely that the Bolsheviks would use the Cheka in the struggle with their left-wing opponents which reached its height that summer over the issue of the peace. The Left Communists did not play an active role in this; in the interests of party unity they had merely abstained from voting on the ratification of the treaty at the congress of Soviets on 16 March, and although Bukharin at first gained some support in Moscow, he and his followers had no wish to join forces with the other factions. The Left Social Revolutionaries, however, did vote against ratification and this brought an end to their working alliance with the Bolsheviks; they resigned from *Sovnarkom* and continued to raise the cry of a people's revolutionary war against Germany. The Right Social Revolutionaries went still further in advocating the enlisting of aid from the entente Powers, and by the late spring they were building up an open resistance to the Bolsheviks in the region of the Don and in Siberia (see p. 55). It was consequently not surprising that on 14 June their delegates should be expelled from the central executive committee, together with Martov and his Mensheviks.

The climax came during the fifth congress of Soviets at the beginning of July in Moscow. The Left Social Revolutionaries were present in some strength – 352 against 745 Bolsheviks – and when Trotsky demanded an end to unofficial partisan attacks on the Germans now established in the Ukraine, he was shouted down. Then on 6 July the Left Social Revolutionaries made their bid to wreck the peace with Germany, when two of their members assassinated the newly-appointed German ambassador Count von Mirbach at his embassy. Dzerzhinsky, rushing round to the headquarters of the Left Social Revolutionary Cheka troops, was promptly taken prisoner and his captors declared: 'the Brest-Litovsk treaty is torn up; war with Germany is unavoidable' (**54**). All this, however, was more of a demonstration than a coup and the Bolsheviks made short work of it in Moscow and Petrograd. The Social Revolutionary delegates at the congress were all arrested and Lenin hastened to the German embassy to express his regrets personally. At the same time the crushing of a Right Social Revolutionary insurrection at Yaroslav was followed by the execution of some 350, and at Nizhny-Novgorod there were 700 arrests.

Soon the Bolshevik leaders themselves were to come under fire. On 30 August Uritsky was killed in Petrograd and Lenin was seriously wounded when he was shot down in the street in Moscow. To this the central executive committee of the Soviets responded by announcing an uncompromising policy of terror. In Petrograd 800 people, including several Tsarist ministers, paid with their lives for the death of Uritsky and throughout the provinces there was a holocaust of executions, as prisoners and hostages were tortured and shot by the Cheka. The western Powers, too, were accused of complicity; Bruce Lockhart, acting as the unofficial British representative, was arrested, and the British naval attaché was killed in an encounter with the Cheka at the embassy in Petrograd (**17**).

The Bolsheviks now seemed locked in a full scale war with their Socialist rivals, however much they might talk about bourgeois subversion, but by the summer of 1918 a greater threat had appeared. The forces of the right – the Whites – were at last beginning to mass. In the face of this the left agreed temporarily to sink their differences, and in November the Mensheviks were allowed back into the central executive committee, to be followed by the Social Revolutionaries in February 1919. The struggle for survival had now entered on its next phase.

6 Civil War and its Consequences: 1918–1921

The Course of the War

The initial resistance to the Bolshevik coup had begun early in 1918 after a number of Tsarist generals, including Kornilov, Denikin and Krasnov, had made their way south in the hope of organizing an army in the area of Rostov and the Kuban with the aid of the Don Cossacks. Their forces were tiny and they were at first hard pressed by Bolshevik troops who were also in action against the Ukrainian nationalists. The evacuation of the Ukraine by the Bolsheviks after the treaty of Brest-Litovsk brought some relief, however, and by June amid a confusion of local Soviets and a German occupation the Whites had mustered an army of some 9,000 under Denikin, who had assumed command after Kornilov's death in April (**88**).

An entirely separate danger was represented by the activities of 30,000 Czechs, who had been released from Russian prisoner-of-war camps through the negotiations of Professor Masaryk, the Czech national leader, on the understanding that they would join the western Allies in France. In May 1918, in the course of their journey across Siberia, they fell out with local Bolshevik groups and were soon in possession of the whole of the Trans-Siberian railway from just west of the Urals to Vladivostok. On 8 June they seized Samara, and the Right Social Revolutionaries, whose influence was strong in the region, created a new government under a committee consisting of local members of the Constituent Assembly. In Manchuria this had the support of General Horvath, the manager of the Chinese eastern railway, who had already established his own local governmental committee. In July the Czechs took Simbirsk and advanced on Ekaterinburg, whereupon the Bolshevik defenders murdered Tsar Nicholas and his family who had been in custody there. In August an all-party conference at Ufa set up a coalition Directory of five and the finances of this new anti-Bolshevik government were almost at once enormously strengthened by the capture of the imperial gold reserve at Kazan (*see* map p. 58).

Meanwhile, there were other dangers closer at hand. By the end of April the Finnish Whites under General Mannerheim had defeated the local Bolsheviks and the Karelian frontier was only a stone's throw from Petrograd. South of the Gulf Estonian nationalists were also resisting the local Soviets. To the north an Allied expeditionary force had landed at Murmansk in April to prevent military stores there from falling into the hands of the Germans, and on their arrival at Archangel in August found that the Whites had already taken over the town. Thus by the late summer of 1918 it seemed that the Bolshevik government in Moscow was hopelessly ringed by foes.

In March 1918 a Supreme Military Council had already been formed under Trotsky as commissar for war (**80, 86**). With only a few thousand Red Guards, a Latvian rifle regiment and one or two other units at their disposal it was clear that the first essential was the creation of a new army. This involved the abandonment of several earlier assumptions. Like most of the left the Bolsheviks had had a vague idea of the whole people in arms acting in defence of the revolution. An appeal for volunteers, however, produced little response and from May 1918 recruiting was based on conscription, initially from the factories whose workers were thought to be more reliable than the peasantry. By April 1919 the Red Army numbered half a million and even allowing for countless desertions this had risen to five million by June 1920. The election of officers was abolished and Trotsky had little time for the irregular bands of partisans operating in the western regions. Instead he exercised a centralized command through war Soviets with each revolutionary army, as he moved from front to front in the train that served him as mobile headquarters. The presence of 180,000 party members provided a stiffening at every level, and local commissars and the Cheka were responsible for a strict supervision down to the smallest military unit. Trotsky's most controversial measure was the employment of some 48,000 former Tsarist officers. Left Communists and Left Social Revolutionaries strongly objected to this, but Trotsky, like Lenin in his handling of the factories, was not prepared to let doctrine stand in the way of using all available expertise and even made one of them, Colonel Vatzetis, commander of the entire eastern front. It was a calculated risk; commissars watched them at every step and their families were held hostage, but perhaps the greatest danger for Trotsky lay in the opportunity that his policy offered to his rivals, such as Stalin, to undermine him in the eyes of Lenin.

In the summer of 1918 the immediate threat lay in the two theatres in the south and the east, since Denikin's forces around Tsaritsyn had already cut off Moscow's sole remaining source of food from the northern Caucasus and looked as if they might link up with the Czechs who now held Kazan. Trotsky set off for the Upper Volga in his command train, instilled a new fighting spirit with the use of his firing squads and by the end of September had won back Kazan and Simbirsk as well as Samara and Ufa later in the year. Meanwhile, Stalin at Tsaritsyn had ensured that its besiegers were driven off, but by now the quarrel between him and Trotsky had flared up – nominally over Trotsky's choice of a Tsarist officer as commander of the southern army – and eventually, in order to placate Trotsky, Lenin recalled Stalin to Moscow.

This, however, was a purely personal feud. In Siberia their opponents were harassed by a much more serious political division. The Social Revolutionaries, whose leader Chernov had joined them in August, lost control of the anti-Bolshevik government set up after the Ufa conference and in November more conservative elements suppressed the Directory of five and appointed a Russian naval officer, Admiral Kolchak, as supreme ruler.

Nevertheless, despite these internal difficulties the Whites were able to launch three entirely separate offensives in 1919, each of which appeared momentarily as if it might bring victory. In the east Kolchak had taken Perm in December 1918 and in the following spring he recaptured Ufa. After this, however, his forces failed to concentrate their attack. By April the Red Army was pushing back towards the Urals and was soon in pursuit of Kolchak, capturing Ekaterinburg in July and Omsk in November. In the south Denikin began an advance northwards in May. Kharkov and Tsaritsyn fell to him in June, Poltava in July, Kiev in August and by October the capture of Chernigov and Orel had brought him within 400 kilometres of Moscow. By now, however, his strength was spent and after a counter-attack by the Red Army near Orel the White retreat began. Meanwhile, in the west General Yudenich had advanced from Estonia on Petrograd in May and after an initial repulse renewed the attack in October. The situation became so serious that Lenin believed that it would be necessary to abandon the city, but Trotsky was determined to resist and, after taking charge of its defence, proved his point by driving Yudenich off in the space of a week.

The year 1920 saw the final success of the Red Army. Kolchak, who had moved back to Irkutsk near Lake Baikal, was handed over

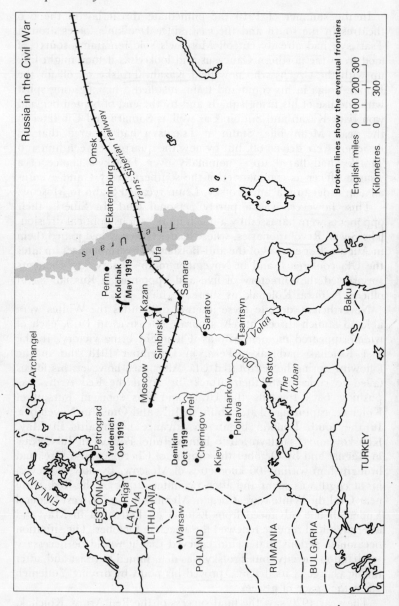

Russia in the Civil War

Broken lines show the eventual frontiers

English miles 0 100 200 300

Kilometres 0 300

Archangel

Petrograd
Yudenich Oct 1919

FINLAND

ESTONIA
Riga
LATVIA
LITHUANIA

Warsaw

POLAND

RUMANIA

BULGARIA

Moscow

Orel
Chernigov
Denikin Oct 1919
Kiev
Kharkov
Poltava

Rostov

The Kuban

TURKEY

Trans-Siberian railway
Omsk

Ekaterinburg

Perm
Kolchak May 1919

The Urals

Ufa

Kazan
Simbirsk
Samara
Saratov
Tsaritsyn

Volga

Don

Baku

to the Bolsheviks by his own troops and shot. In the south Wrangel, who had taken over from Denikin, was unable to check the Bolshevik invasion of the Crimea. In April the Poles entered the struggle with an advance into the Ukraine, but were soon repulsed and by August the Red Army had reached the outskirts of Warsaw. Here, however, a new Polish offensive drove them back some 480 kilometres to a line which the peace of Riga in March 1921 finally established as the new frontier, still leaving the Russians in possession of the Ukraine.

There are many factors that explain the Bolshevik victory in the civil war. The forces of the Whites had been scattered around the perimeter of Russia, separated by vast distances that precluded concerted action. Politically they were divided amongst themselves and got little cooperation from the local peasant population who, although treated atrociously by both sides, regarded the Whites as the landlord class. The western Powers were too exhausted and preoccupied with the defeat of Germany to do much for them, and the Whites' refusal to recognize the independence of Finland, Estonia and Latvia deprived them of the support of those states whose geographical position could have helped them considerably. In contrast to this, the Bolsheviks had interior lines, the use of railways and above all a fanatical unity of purpose which enabled them to impose a ferocious discipline on their war effort remote from the bickering of their opponents.

War Communism

Throughout the war the occupation of large territories by the Whites, coupled with the devastation in the subsequent fighting, had presented the Bolsheviks with appalling problems of supply. Until 1920 they were cut off from the coal in the area of the Don, from the iron ore of the Urals and the Ukraine, and from the oil at Baku which was occupied by the Turks. In the production of cast-iron alone output had dropped by 1919 to a third of what it had been in 1918, and by 1920 to less than a twelfth, and the international blockade made it impossible to remedy any of these deficiencies from abroad. To meet its immediate expenses the government printed off masses of paper money and in the resulting inflation the value of the rouble had fallen by October 1920 to one per cent of what it had been at the time of the Bolshevik coup. This enormously magnified the problem of food production which had harassed the Tsarist government before 1917 (see p. 23). The peasant, unable to purchase goods from the towns and unwilling to save worthless notes, resorted increasingly to subsistence farming, and the consequent shortage of food in the cities became so severe that nearly a third of the urban population moved out into the countryside. By 1919 three-quarters of the wages of an industrial worker was being paid in meagre rations (**85**).

The extension of state control over every aspect of the economy was an obvious response to these desperate circumstances, although doctrinaire Communists also saw this as a natural realization of their ideal. All forms of trade and distribution became a state monopoly. In industry large and medium-sized concerns serving a national market were brought under the *Glavki*, the subordinate bodies of *Vesenkha* (see p. 48), while smaller ones were supervised by provincial economic councils. By 1920 37,000 enterprises involving more than 1.5 million workers had been nationalized. All this was accompanied by an immense mushrooming of bureaucracy which Lenin attempted to combat by reducing the independence of the provincial economic councils and drawing the *Glavki* closer to *Vesenkha* in a greater centralization. At the same time in the interests of efficiency he pressed on with the policy of replacing local committees with single managers. Both of these developments were deplored by Communist idealists who pointed out that the influence of trade unions and factory committees was being undermined by the *Glavki*, whose members were increasingly drawn from the old bourgeois managerial class (**53**).

A Commissariat of Supplies (*Narkomprod*) was made responsible for the feeding of the cities and the army. In 1918 the immediate method was to organize committees of poor peasants in the villages and detachments of armed workers from the towns, both of whom were to extract grain from the kulaks. The furore of requisitioning that ensued soon seemed likely to antagonize the large class of middle peasants and might upset the partnership of proletariat and peasantry that Lenin was determined to create. Accordingly, in January 1919 the onus of collection was transferred to the smallest rural units on a basis of stipulated quotas. This proved a more acceptable system, although the peasant still had to hand over everything that was surplus to his personal requirements. Lenin was aware that the long-term essential was larger units of agricultural production, but collective farms were a sensitive issue and the 3,100 that had been established in 1918 had only cautiously been increased to 4,400 by 1920. In the main, however, all these methods did at least ensure a food supply of about one-third of the pre-war level in the towns, as well as enabling the government to feed an army that eventually numbered five million.

N.E.P.

By the autumn of 1920, when Wrangel was finally driven from the Crimea and an armistice had been signed with the Poles, it was clear that the Bolshevik government had survived all attacks. It was equally clear that the country which they ruled lay in ruin. Industrial output was minimal, railway rolling stock was worn out and economic life rested on a primitive system of barter. To avoid requisitioning, the peasantry were sowing secretly in distant scattered strips – as much as 50 million hectares, it was reckoned by 1920 – and the failure of any satisfactory system of distribution was soon to lead to an appalling famine in the south.

Furthermore, the end of the civil war now allowed a revival of internal hostility to the regime. Sporadic peasant revolt was accompanied by unrest among the party members themselves. There was strong criticism of the bureaucratic centralism exercised by the central committee and a growing dislike of Trotsky's plans to extend the discipline of the Red Army to the civilian work force to bring about the immediate rehabilitation of Russia. By the end of 1920 Menshevik representation in the local Soviets was sharply increasing and a Workers' Opposition under Shliapnikov was decrying the subordination of the trade unions, who objected to their committees being nominated from above.

The climax of all these discontents came in March 1921 when the sailors in Kronstadt – by now mostly conscripted Ukrainian peasants – rose in revolt, demanding an end to the special position of the Bolshevik party, a relaxation of economic controls and the restoration of freedom of speech and association for all Socialists. Naturally revolt had to be suppressed and Trotsky, who had once described Kronstadt as 'the pride and the glory of the revolution' (**80**), took charge of the operation in which the defenders of the island fortress were ruthlessly massacred. Lenin called the Kronstadt rising the 'flash that lit up reality better than anything' (**77**), but he had himself already seen the need for a radical change of policy, and the principal significance of 'the flash' was that it enabled him to overcome any opposition to his proposals at the tenth party congress which was meeting at the same time as the revolt.

The most startling feature of the New Economic Policy (N.E.P.)

that he now introduced was that it restored a limited system of private enterprise [**doc. 15**]. Initially this abandonment of war communism was centred on the peasantry. The amount of farm produce to be requisitioned was reduced and they were to be allowed freedom to trade with the surplus. The implications of this were enormous. It meant not merely a return to a money economy and the probable re-establishment of the kulaks; it demanded also, as Lenin realized, a similar freedom of trade for the factories which supplied the shops in the cities where the peasant would wish to make his purchases. Thus the monopolistic control exercised by *Vesenkha* through its *Glavki* would have to be relaxed, and in the autumn of 1921 all concerns producing consumer goods were allowed to make their own arrangements for obtaining their materials and organizing their markets. Within a year 3,800 nationalized enterprises had been leased out and by 1923 the private trader, the *Nepman*, had captured half the market between factory, shop and peasant.

Lenin claimed that all this could take place within the framework of state capitalism. The government held the commanding heights of heavy industry, banking and foreign trade, and *Vesenkha* still exercised a certain supervision over the trusts formed by groups of independent factories. Nevertheless, he was well aware of the possible political consequences of what he was doing. After 1921 traders, shopkeepers and farmers making use of hired labour were all operating a bourgeois economy out of which a new rich class might well emerge. Thus, since Marxism declared that forms of government were a superstructure erected in the interest of the class that held economic power, it should follow from this that they would eventually oust the Bolshevik party with governmental institutions of their own. Lenin, naturally, had no intention of allowing that to happen, and as a consequence the Bolshevik regime had to be buttressed against the very tendencies that Marxism regarded as inescapable. He was in effect standing Marxism on its head, since the basis of power was now to be the political structure rather than the economic order.

To achieve this, the Bolsheviks had to be forced to close ranks, and at the party congress in March 1921 he made it clear that they could no longer afford the luxury of factional debate, which until then had been permitted to some degree in the upper levels of their organization. This was particularly aimed at the Workers' Opposition groups who still wanted greater independence for the trade unions despite some concessions over the election of their committees. The weapon was to be the right of the Bolshevik central committee to expel anyone from the party – including members of the central committee itself, provided that there was a two-thirds majority for this. 'Let the central committee in a moment of danger,' declared Radek, 'take the severest measure against the best party comrade, if it finds this necessary' (**66**). And obviously if there was to be no toleration of dissentient views within the party, it was hardly likely that there would be any for the groups outside it. Martov himself had already gone to Germany in the autumn of 1920, and in 1921 the Mensheviks were simply encouraged to leave the country. The Social Revolutionaries were less fortunate and in 1922 thirty-four of the leaders were put on trial and twelve were condemned to death.

N.E.P. certainly enabled Russia to make an economic recovery, but, it does not seem that Lenin was entirely satisfied with its working, and, had he lived, the subsequent policy of enforced collectivization of farms and industrial Five Year Plans might have been introduced earlier than it was. In May 1922, however, he suffered the first of a series of strokes, and when he died in January 1924, the contradictions of Socialism and capitalism were still unresolved.

Part Three: Assessment

The essential factor in the story of the Bolshevik revolution was the collapse of the Tsarist government in February 1917. But for this, Lenin might well have ended his days as a frustrated émigré, perhaps taking up chess again in his old age. It is easy, of course, to argue from hindsight that this collapse was bound to come, but the indications are by no means sure. The regime had survived the 1905 revolution; the reforms of Stolypin had been an intelligent response to the backwardness of Russian peasant society and although the left-wing organizations had remained active, the Tsarist police were clearly skilful at infiltrating them. Not even Russia's military performance in the war had suggested an imminent breakdown, and as late as January 1917 Lenin commented in a lecture in Switzerland: 'we of the older generation may not see the decisive battles of the coming revolution' (**74**). Nevertheless, within a few weeks the strains and tensions of war had brought about that odd sequence of events in which the multiplicity of political ambitions and the disillusionment of the generals combined to turn a local upheaval in Petrograd into a revolution.

Thus unexpectedly the stage was set for Lenin's eventual success. Yet in the spring of 1917 the Bolshevik party was only a tiny element on the political scene and the failure of any alternative regime to survive still has to be explained. Why, for example, were the Liberals unable to consolidate the revolution, as the Mensheviks expected them to do? In broad terms one may argue that their social basis was too narrow; the industrial changes in Russia had been too recent for a large managerial class to have developed and the extent of their political experience was inadequate for them to be able to exploit the opportunity when it came. All this was as Trotsky had predicted, but there were also various political difficulties. For many of the Liberals the objective had been the transference of political power to themselves without bringing about a major disruption of existing society, and in the nineteenth century their counterparts in western Europe had usually hoped to achieve this through the establishment of constitutional monarchies. It is just possible that massive concessions by Nicholas during the February days might have enabled them to hold the situation in check, before disaffection among the troops had spread beyond the Petrograd garrison, but Nicholas's determination to cling to the autocracy ruled this out. Instead, the upper-class Liberals, taking the conservatives somewhat unwillingly with them, were faced with the far more indeterminate prospect of a republic in which the presence of the Petrograd Soviet in the Tauride Palace seemed to make social change inescapable.

In the event the Soviet turned out to be less aggressive than it had at first appeared, and conceivably the Liberals could still have stabilized their position. What prevented them was the continuation of the war. This undermined all governments between February and October 1917, since it diverted their energies and put a brake on an active domestic policy. If there could have been an immediate armistice, a vast demobilization might have averted the growing indiscipline in the army; the government would have been left with a smaller, more reliable force, and the election of the Constituent Assembly and some settlement of the land question could have been speeded up. But Russia was dependent on the Allies for recognition and financial support; Liberals like Milyukov had no wish to give up the chance of gaining the Straits as promised in the secret treaties, and in the subsequent coalition governments the Socialists, even though they wanted no annexations, also believed in the need to resist Germany – as they still did at the time of Brest-Litovsk. Thus the war dragged on and the sense of impatience engendered by the apparent inertia on the domestic front opened the door to a growing anarchy in the countryside that was too much for successive governments whose authority was so insecurely established. And throughout those months the discipline of the army itself was eroded by the propaganda of left-wing agitators and news sheets and the activity of the soldiers' councils – to such an extent that it is hard to visualize any moment shortly after February 1917 when a right-wing military coup would have been possible. In these circumstances there was nothing very remarkable about the October revolution. As one historian has said, the Bolsheviks did not seize power; they picked it up (**74**).

Lenin was also assisted by the hesitancy of the other Socialist parties. Despite the practical control that the Petrograd Soviet could exercise, the furthest that they would go was to join the Liberals in a provisional coalition while awaiting the election of the Constituent Assembly; the Mensheviks could argue that the time was not yet ripe for a Socialist government, but the principal reason was that none of them had any confidence in their ability to rule Russia on their own. 'It makes you giddy,' admitted Lenin, when he emerged from hiding into political power in October, and the other Socialist groups clearly felt the same after the February days. The whole thing happened too quickly and as a consequence in the summer of that year Petrograd seemed to be littered with left-wing revolutionaries who did not know what to do with a revolution. 'At the present moment there is no political party which would say: "give the power into our hands",' said the Menshevik Tseretelli at the first All-Russian congress in June (**53**), and Lenin's comment that there was one merely provoked mocking laughter. Only Kerensky seemed to regard coalition as a positive policy for bridging the gulf between left and right, but he could rely on little more than his own rhetoric to achieve this and by the autumn of 1917 his position was hopelessly isolated. The masses had by then moved far to the left of him; he had lost the support of the Socialist leaders in the pre-Parliament, and when he turned to the generals on 25 October, he found that they saw him as the enemy of Kornilov; as a consequence he could collect only a handful of troops at a moment when the Bolshevik forces in Petrograd could hardly have withstood a sustained attack.

The ultimate question is: why did the other Socialists remain so blind to the possibility of a Bolshevik coup? The reason was that they regarded the conservative interest as their main antagonist; counter-revolution was the predominant fear, heightened by the thought that failure here would probably mean their own execution. Consequently the Bolsheviks might arouse a sense of irritation and occasionally alarm, but most Socialists still saw them fundamentally as their comrades, as allies against the right. This explains both the relative mildness with which the government treated them after the July days and the speed with which they welcomed them back during the Kornilov crisis. In any case, the other Socialist groups' refusal to believe that any of them could rule alone also influenced their attitude; they were sure that even if the Bolsheviks did take power, they would be unable to cope with the problems of government and would have to give up after a few days – hence the continuing demand for a left-wing coalition after the October coup, which, as has been seen, did appeal to some members of the Bolshevik central committee.

All these external factors helped in varying degrees to make it possible to establish the Bolshevik regime; none of them would by itself have brought it about. That was essentially the work of Lenin. The key to his success did not lie primarily in a different interpretation of Marxism, although his was certainly different; nor on the sureness of his political instinct, although this too was outstanding. What distinguished him from the other Socialist leaders was his conception of the party [**doc. 3**] which he had outlined in his pamphlet *What is to be done?* and which had led to the Bolshevik-Menshevik split at the Russian Social Democrat congress in 1903 in Brussels. However radical the attitude of the non-Bolshevik Socialists, they all believed in a free exchange of debate in which compromise with the minority groups might eventually lead to a majority decision – in fact, the parliamentary processes for which Lenin had supreme contempt. In contrast to them Lenin believed that the opportunity offered by the revolution could be grasped by a small dedicated élite whose discipline would enable them to act decisively when the moment came.

This, at least, is one interpretation of his efforts. It has, however, been argued that the conception of the small élite really belongs to the conspiratorial period, and that by the summer of 1917 the enormous growth in the size of the Bolshevik party made such a tight control virtually impossible. The confusion over the July days and the difficulty that Lenin had in persuading his party to seize power might well seem to illustrate this, and it has been suggested that much of the Bolsheviks' strength actually derived from a freedom of debate at various levels of the party machine (**65**).

If this is so, it would be reasonable to ask why such freedom was not of similar assistance to the Mensheviks and Social Revolutionaries. In fact, the distinguishing feature of the Bolsheviks was not the luxury of debate, but Lenin's dynamic will in creating his own organization, dominating it and preventing dilution through participation in government with other groups. In its central committee he had only the power of persuasion and invective to drive the other members to accept his view, and only one final weapon, the threat to resign – which could be effective, since it was clear that there was no one comparable to replace him, except possibly Trotsky, who had only joined the party in 1917. It was with this instrument that he intended to gain power so as to establish what he called the revolutionary democratic dictatorship of the proletariat and peasantry. To achieve this he was prepared ruthlessly to encourage the growing anarchy of 1917, at the same time building up his own force of Red Guards. He did not care how he gained money for the party – from bank robberies before the war, from Germany in 1917 [**doc. 6a**]. And once in power he did not hesitate to use the machinery of state and a policy of terror to quell the anarchy which had put him there. In all this the Bolsheviks were unique.

With this relentless sense of purpose Lenin combined a flexibility of political manoeuvre which his colleagues sometimes found difficult to follow. The April theses had come as a surprise to many of them, but even these were merely tactical points from which he was quite prepared to depart. In April he spoke out positively in favour of the nationalization of land. Yet when by the autumn it was clear that the peasantry were determined to seize their own individual holdings, the land decree of 26 October openly presented them with the Social Revolutionary programme and gave only the faintest hint of eventual nationalization. Equally in April he raised the cry of 'all power to the Soviets', but when in July 1917 the Petrograd Soviet and the central executive committee under its Menshevik leadership rejected the demands of the crowd to take power, he promptly abandoned it. 'That slogan has patently ceased to be correct now' (**6**), he declared, and in August, from his hiding place thirty kilometres from Petrograd, he steered a somewhat confused Bolshevik party congress towards proclaiming instead a reliance upon the revolutionary proletariat. Of course, by the time of the second All-Russian congress of Soviets in October, when he reckoned to have a majority, he had swung back again, although the difference of view between Lenin and Trotsky over the timing of the coup suggests that Trotsky envisaged a closer conjunction with the Soviets than Lenin did.

The quickness of response to immediate circumstances is still more noticeable after he had gained power. This did enable his one-party government to survive, but it is appropriate to ask whether his various manoeuvres and improvisations may not finally have created a situation very different from what he had initially imagined. In September 1917 he had put forward those aims in a long essay *State and Revolution*, in which he quoted extensively from Marx and Engels, although there was much, too, that was reminiscent of Tkachev. Since he clearly regarded this essay as an important statement of principle, it may serve as a convenient yardstick to set against the eventual nature of the Bolshevik government. The conclusions that have been drawn from such a comparison, however, are by no means unanimous; one writer reckons that 'it would be a fundamental error to suppose that the experience of power brought any radical change in Lenin's philosophy of the state' (**53**), while another finds the divergence so great that he describes the essay as 'a source of bafflement and irritation to his official commentators' (**74**).

In certain respects *State and Revolution* is a guarded prognosis of what did happen [**doc. 7**]. The bourgeois system was to be destroyed by physical force, but the dictatorship of the proletariat that succeeded it would need to retain the apparatus of the state for some time in order to root out the relics of the bourgeois outlook. Thus in the first phase of a Communist society the new attitudes would still have to be enforced by an external authority. It was only when those attitudes had become automatic that the second higher phase of Communism would have been achieved and the state would then wither away. Once in power Lenin was emphatic that the attainment of this second phase might take some considerable time. 'To proclaim this withering away in advance,' he was saying as early as March 1918, 'is to violate historical perspective' (**53**), but this did not particularly contradict *State and Revolution*, since he had been careful not to give a precise date for the moment when the state would begin to wither away. 'There is no material for an answer to these questions' (**6**).

There are nevertheless certain aspects of *State and Revolution* that later events did belie. He had been remarkably optimistic in predicting that there would be no problem in taking over the whole structure of capitalist society. 'All citizens become employees and workers of a single national state syndicate. All that is required is that they should work equally, do their proper share of work and get paid equally. The accounting and control necessary for this has been simplified by capitalism and reduced to the extraordinary simple operations – which any literate person can perform – of checking and recording, knowledge of the four rules of arithmetic and issuing receipts' (**6**). And in his speech to the Petrograd Soviet on the afternoon of 25 October 1917 he declared: 'we shall establish genuine workers' control over production' (**53**).

A few months after the October revolution all this had changed. In industry the factory committees were hopeless from the start. The Supreme Council of National Economy (*Vesenkha*), established on 2 December 1917, was largely designed to supersede them, and the trades unions, whom Lenin had always mistrusted, proved a useful ally for the government against them. Even the ownership of industry by the state was largely nominal, and although it exercised supervision the detailed administration had to be left to the former managers and specialists [**doc. 12a**]. This recognition of the need for expertise was openly acknowledged by Lenin at the third congress of Soviets in January 1918. 'There was not a single man in our group who imagined that such a cunning delicate apparatus as that of banking, developed in the course of centuries out of the capitalist system of production, could be broken or made over in a few days' (**53**). To judge from *State and Revolution*, however, it seems that there had at least been one man who had imagined it.

The fundamental misconception in the essay lay in his belief that the authority still needed during the first phase of Communism would be achieved by 'the simple organization of the armed masses' – a kind of general will so overwhelming that it would accomplish everything with a minimum of external control. The type of state power that emerged in Russia after 1917, however, made nonsense of this dream. As in industry, the work of government was seen increasingly as a specialist function. 'Can any worker administer the state?' he asked a labour union meeting in 1921. 'Practical people know that this is fantasy' (**74**). The organization of the armed masses had turned into the coercing of the peasantry, the instituting of labour camps for the recalcitrant, the mass executions by the Cheka and a labyrinthine development of the bureaucracy, all of which weighed as heavily upon the classes whom it was supposed to liberate as it did upon representatives of the old order. A new autocracy had emerged, far more ruthless than the one which it had replaced, and the Kronstadt rising in March 1921 was the ultimate comment on that.

His Menshevik opponents maintained that this was not simply due to the dictates of expediency. It was the inevitable outcome of Lenin's whole policy of speeding up the historical process through the capture of power by a small revolutionary group. In their view the proletarian revolution in Russia should only have taken place many years after the bourgeois state had established a fully developed industrial economy, within which a numerous working class of highly skilled technicians would have had generations of political experience through parliamentary activity and trade union negotiation. Then, and only then, would the time be ripe for the proletariat to take over and at last to inherit the earth. But in 1917 the only earth to inherit was being seized by the peasantry; the whole framework of a sophisticated bourgeois economy had still to be created and in attempting to supply this deficiency a Socialist government in the hands of a party such as Lenin's was bound eventually to establish a dictatorship. Once again the thread runs back to the great debate that had raged since 1903. The Mensheviks may not have proved very effective men of action in

1917, but their intellectual analysis of Lenin's policy was nevertheless shown to be highly accurate.

Ironically the two main protagonists of the October coup had themselves in earlier years expressed reservations that were to be extremely prophetic. Lenin never wavered over the need for a disciplined party, but he had not originally envisaged it dictating to the masses. 'Whoever wants to approach Socialism by any other path than that of political democracy,' he wrote in 1905, 'will inevitably arrive at absurd and reactionary conclusions both economic and political' (**83**). Trotsky, on the other hand, had had no doubt that the party of the proletariat must lead the way in Russia, where the bourgeois class was too weak to accomplish its own stage of revolution; what he had disliked was Lenin's conception of the party itself. 'Lenin's methods lead to this,' he wrote in 1904; 'the party organization at first substitutes itself for the party as a whole; then the central committee substitutes itself for the organization; and finally a single dictator substitutes himself for the central committee' (**80**). But by 1917 they had each silenced their misgivings and had joined forces to create a government in which the disciplined party would impose its own solution upon the whole of Russia.

Even so, they were aware that they were forcing the pace. Lenin himself in the April theses had admitted that Russia was not yet ready for Socialism in its classical form: 'our immediate task is not to introduce Socialism, but only to bring social production and distribution of products at once under the control of the Soviets of Workers' Deputies' (**6**). This might seem an open acknowledgement of the Menshevik criticism that he was acting prematurely. The Bolshevik answer was based on the view which Marx had expressed in later life (see p. 10). If their coup became the signal for an upheaval which would establish Socialism throughout Europe, then in that changed context they felt that the worst aspects of a party dictatorship predicted by the Mensheviks could be averted.

This is why Lenin placed such emphasis on the imminence of a general revolution when he had to counter the objections of Zinoviev and Kamenev at that secret meeting of the Bolshevik central committee on 10 October 1917. In fact, Zinoviev and Kamenev were proved correct in their doubts, and it is intriguing to wonder how far Lenin himself was entirely convinced on this score. Only a few days before he had written: 'we do not know how soon after our victory the revolution in the west will come' (**66**), but it would only have been human if he had refused to let intellectual theorizing stand in his way at a moment when, after so many years of conspiracy, power was at last within his reach.

At least, whatever his true views in October may have been, he seems to have recognized remarkably quickly that the hopes for general revolution were to be disappointed – hence his acceptance of the terms of Brest-Litovsk. This meant also abandoning the programme of the Zimmerwald Left which he had headed in 1915 – the idea that, once revolution had come in Russia, it would be necessary to fight a people's war in alliance with the Socialists of central Europe. By the beginning of 1918 he knew that this was not feasible and there is little doubt that he was right [**doc. 11**]. The German army would have been a very different proposition to the confused and divided elements with which Trotsky's Red Army had to contend in the civil war. Nevertheless, the extent to which this decision flouted accepted doctrine may be measured by the fury that it aroused among the Left Communists and the Social Revolutionaries.

The likelihood of European revolution was not much greater even after November 1918. The Central Powers had suffered the traumatic shock of defeat, but, unlike the provisional governments in Russia in 1917, the regimes which emerged after the fall of the German and Austrian monarchies did not have to cope with the strain of fighting a war (**84, 97**). Their civil administrations were undamaged; their middle classes were strongly entrenched and their Social Democrat movements, far from warming to Lenin's action, tended to move towards a greater reliance on parliamentary processes. What revolution there was in central Europe was narrowly political, not social – the aim of the Duma Liberals in March 1917. Thus the essential condition which alone was supposed to justify the revolution of October 1917 remained unfulfilled and Bolshevik Russia was left in a state of siege in which the party was bound to strengthen its grip, if it was to accomplish anything at all.

The civil war did much to consolidate this, but the final step was taken as a result of Lenin's most startling volte-face – the introduction of N.E.P. Although the party retained control over heavy industry and foreign trade, the return to a system of free enterprise in the sale of agricultural goods and the products of light industry meant that a largely bourgeois economy was now being reintroduced as an essential preliminary to the development of state capitalism and thence Socialism. This was more than an

acknowledgement that the Bolshevik revolution had been premature. It created a doctrinal anomaly in that the economic order was
at variance with the political system and this could well have led
on to the classic pattern of revolution, in which the excitement and
optimism of the early days are succeeded by a right-wing reaction.
So far, this had been averted – in 1917, with the undermining of
Kornilov, if indeed it had been his intention then to head such a
movement, and, later, with the defeat of the Whites in the civil war.
Thus now, the temporary retreat into private enterprise had to be
buttressed with firm controls and this brought about the final
consolidating of the party committee as the supreme authority in
Russia – a position which would be still more emphasized when the
time came to abandon N.E.P. with the forcible imposition of agricultural collectivization and the industrial five-year plans. The
penultimate stage of Trotsky's prediction in 1904 had now been
reached – 'the central committee substitutes itself for the organization' – and the eventual emergence of the dictatorship of Stalin
and the political terror, in which so many of the original Bolsheviks
were to perish, can be seen not as the perversion of Lenin's work,
but as the natural consequence of it.

Part Four: Documents

The Communist Manifesto

*The manifesto was composed by Karl Marx and Friedrich Engels early in
1848 at the request of the congress of the Communist League held in London
in November 1847. The original German version was published in London
at the time of the revolution in Paris and was soon translated into most
European languages, although not into Russian until 1863.*

The history of all hitherto existing society is the history of class
struggles. Freeman and slave, patrician and plebeian, lords,
vassals, guild-masters, journeymen, apprentices, serfs; oppressor
and oppressed, stood in constant opposition to one another, carried
on an uninterrupted, now hidden, now open fight, a fight that each
time ended, either in a revolutionary reconstitution of society at
large, or in the common ruin of the contending class.

In the earlier epochs of history, we find almost everywhere a
complicated arrangement of society into various orders, a manifold
gradation of social rank. In ancient Rome we have patricians,
knights, plebeians, slaves; in the Middle Ages feudal lords, vassals,
guild-masters, journeymen, apprentices, serfs; in almost all of these
classes, again, subordinate gradations.

The modern bourgeois society that has sprouted from the ruins
of feudal society has not done away with class antagonisms. It has
but established new classes, new conditions of oppression, new
forms of struggle in place of the old ones.

Our epoch, the epoch of the bourgeoisie, possesses, however, this
distinctive feature: it has simplified the class antagonisms. Society
as a whole is more and more splitting up into great hostile camps,
into two great classes directly facing each other – bourgeoisie and
proletariat. . . .

The essential condition for the existence and for the sway of the
bourgeois class is the formation and the augmentation of capital;
the condition for capital is wage labour. Wage labour rests exclus-

ively on competition between the labourers. The advance of industry, whose involuntary promoter is the bourgeoisie, replaces the isolation of the labourers, due to competition, by their revolutionary combination, due to association. The development of modern industry, therefore, cuts from under its feet the very foundation on which the bourgeoisie produces and appropriates products. What the bourgeoisie therefore produces, above all, are its own gravediggers. Its fall and the victory of the proletariat are equally inevitable.

The Essential Left (**12**), pp. 14, 26.

document 2
Russian Jacobinism

Peter Tkachev (1844–86) produced the fullest exposition of the views of the Russian Jacobins (see p. 6). Although he did not dispute Marx's general economic interpretation of history, his conception of the particular strategy required for revolution in Russia soon brought him into conflict with both Marx and Engels. Soviet historians at first acknowledged a direct link between Tkachev's writings and Lenin's work, but since the Stalin period have been inclined to deny any connection.

The final aim of the social revolution is the triumph of communism, we must introduce new elements, new factors ... which are inherent exclusively in the socialist outlook of the revolutionary minority. That is why the ideal of this minority, broader and more revolutionary than the popular ideal, has to dominate over the latter during the revolution. The people are incapable of building, upon the ruins of the old, a new world that would be able to move and develop towards the communist ideal; therefore they cannot play any significant or leading part in building this new world. Such a part belongs solely to the revolutionary minority. ...

In its reforming activities the revolutionary minority should not count on the *active* support of the people. The latter's revolutionary role will come to an end the moment they demolish the institutions that directly oppress them, and destroy the tyrants who directly exploit them. ...

But the revolutionary minority must be able also to continue its work of revolutionary destruction in those spheres where it can hardly reckon on the genuine support and assistance of the popular majority. That is why it must possess might, power and authority.

And the greater this might, the firmer and more energetic this power, the fuller and more comprehensive the implementation of the ideas of the social revolution, the easier it will be to avoid a conflict with the conservative elements of the people.

In short, the relationship of the revolutionary minority to the people, and the part played by the latter in the revolution, can be defined as follows: the revolutionary minority, having liberated the people from the grip of fear and terror of the authorities, provide them with the opportunity for demonstrating their destructive revolutionary force. Basing itself upon this force, skilfully guiding it towards the destruction of the immediate enemies of the revolution, the minority thereby demolishes the enemy's entrenched strongholds and deprives it of the means of resistance and counteraction. Then, utilizing its power and its authority, the minority introduces new progressive-communistic elements into the people's life; it will shift the people's life off its age-old foundations, and rejuvenate its ossified and shrivelled forms. . . .

The people can never save themselves. Neither in the present nor in the future could the people, left to themselves, carry out the social revolution. Only we, the revolutionary movement, can do this – and we must do it as soon as possible.

Szamuely, *The Russian Tradition* (**38**), pp. 304–305.

The Conception of the Bolshevik Party
document 3

Lenin's pamphlet What is to be done?, *first published in 1902, has remained a basic text-book in Soviet training institutions. In it Lenin was concerned primarily to combat the tendency towards various forms of revisionism in the Social Democrat movement, and his initial assumption was that 'there can be no revolutionary movement without a revolutionary theory'. That theory was not to depend upon some spontaneous awakening among the masses; nor had it much to do with haphazard negotiations between trade unions and employers. It had to be formulated by a small central group of professional revolutionaries who would ensure an obedience to its general principles and decide on the consequent tactical measures to be carried out at the lower levels of the organization. This conception of the disciplined party, which owed a great deal to the writings of Nechaev and Tkachev (see p. 6), was elaborated more fully in another pamphlet published in the same year:* Letter to a Comrade on our Organizational Tasks.

What was the source of our disagreements? Precisely that the 'Economists' continuously deviate from Social-Democratism to trade unionism in organizational, as well as in political, tasks. The political struggle of Social Democracy is far wider and far more complicated than the economic struggle of the workers against the employers and the government. Exactly in the same way (and as a result of it), the organization of a revolutionary Social Democratic party must inevitably be of a *different kind* from an organization of workers for such a struggle. An organization of workers must be first a trade organization; secondly, it must be as broad as possible; thirdly, it must be as little secret as possible (here and further on I speak, of course, only with autocratic Russia in mind). An organization of revolutionaries, on the contrary, must embrace primarily and chiefly people whose profession consists of revolutionary activity. . . . In the face of this common feature of the members of such an organization, *any distinction between workers and intellectuals must be completely obliterated*, not to speak of differences between separate professions and trades. This organization must inevitably be not very wide and as secret as possible.

By clever people in relation to organization, one must understand – as I have already said more than once – *professional revolutionaries*, irrespective of whether they develop out of students or out of workers. And now I maintain: (1) that no revolutionary movement can be durable without a stable organization of leaders which preserves continuity; (2) that the broader the mass which is spontaneously drawn into the struggle, which forms the basis of the movement and participates in it, the more urgent is the necessity for such an organization, and the more durable this organization must be (because the broader the mass, the easier it is for any demagogue to attract the backward sections of the mass); (3) that such an organization must consist mainly of people who are professionally engaged in revolutionary activities; (4) that, in an autocratic country, the more we *narrow* the membership of such an organization, restricting it only to those who are professionally engaged in revolutionary activities and have received a professional training in the art of struggle against the political police, the more difficult will it be to 'catch' such an organization; and (5) the *wider* will be the category of people, both from the working class and from other classes of society, who will have an opportunity of participating in the movement and actively working in it.

Lenin, *What is to be Done?* (**5**), pp. 132, 144.

document 4

The evening of 27 February 1917

Nikolai Himmer, a political journalist who wrote under the name of Sukhanov, abandoned the Social Revolutionary party after the 1905 revolution and joined Martov's section of the Social Democrats in 1917. Throughout that year he was present in Petrograd where he was in touch with most of the political personalities, and in 1922 he published his eye-witness account of the revolution. In this passage he describes the precariousness of the situation in Petrograd at the moment when the Duma provisional committee and the Petrograd Soviet were being set up (see p. 27).

We met cars and lorries, in which soldiers, workers, students, and young women, some wearing arm-bands, were sitting or standing. God knows where all these came from, where they were rushing to, or with what purpose! But all these passengers were extremely excited, shouting and waving their arms, scarcely aware of what they were doing. Rifles were at the ready, and panicky shooting would have started on the least excuse.

Near the Fontanka we turned towards the Shpalerny and the Sergiyevsky. Quite often shots were heard, sometimes in series. Who was firing, why and at what – no one knew. But the spirit of the groups of workers, middle-class people, and soldiers we met, both armed and unarmed, standing about and moving in various directions, was extraordinarily raised by this.

Arms were visible in great quantities in the hands of the workers. Single soldiers were straggling about in all directions in search of shelter, food and safety. Just as in the Moscow uprising, passers-by started talking to each other, asking what was going on over in one place or whether you could get through to some place else.

It was already dark when we came out on the Liteiny, near the bridge where there had been a skirmish a few hours before between Tsarist and revolutionary troops. To the left the District Court was blazing. Guns had been set up at random near the Sergiyevsky. Ammunition boxes were standing behind them, in what looked to me a disorderly fashion. Something like a barricade could be seen there too. But it was crystal clear to every passer-by that neither guns nor barricades would protect anybody or anything from the slightest onslaught.

One might have despaired. But it was impossible to forget the other side of the picture: the arms at the disposal of the revolutionary people were, in their hands, certainly no protection against any organized force; but *Tsarism lacked that force.*

Sukhanov, *The Russian Revolution 1917* (**23**), pp. 44–45.

document 5
Order No. 1

This Order was drawn up on 1 March 1917 at the request of soldiers of the Petrograd garrison who feared that they might still be accused of mutiny (p. 27). The Executive Committee of the Petrograd Soviet only became aware of it after publication, although it was issued in their name. Sukhanov (see p. 78) describes how it was drawn up by a member of the Committee, Sokolov, but it may well have been devised by a Bolshevik, Bonch-Bruevich, who had offered to publish Izvestiya *for the Soviet at a printing works which he had just seized* (**59**). *The Order was to play a considerable part later in the breakdown of discipline in the Russian army* (**96**).

The Soviet of Workers' and Soldiers' Deputies has resolved:
1. In all companies, battalions, regiments, parks, batteries, squadrons, in the special services of the various military administrations, and on the vessels of the navy, committees of elected representatives from the lower ranks of the above-mentioned military units shall be chosen immediately . . .
4. The orders of the military commission of the State Duma shall be executed only in such cases as they do not conflict with the orders and resolutions of the Soviet of Workers' and Soldiers' Deputies.
5. All kinds of arms, such as rifles, machine-guns, armoured automobiles and others, must be kept at the disposal and under the control of the company and battalion committees and must in no case be turned over to officers, even at their demand.
6. In the ranks and during their performance of the duties of the service, soldiers must observe the strictest military discipline, but outside the service and the ranks, in their political, general civic, and private lives, soldiers cannot in any way be deprived of those rights that all citizens enjoy. In particular, standing at attention and compulsory saluting, when not on duty, are abolished.
7. Also, the addressing of the officers with the titles "Your Excellency," "Your Honour," and the like, is abolished, and these titles are replaced by the address of "Mr. General," "Mr.

Colonel," and so forth. Rudeness towards soldiers of any rank, and, especially, addressing them as "thou", is prohibited, and soldiers are required to bring to the attention of the company committees every infraction of this rule, as well as all mis-understandings occurring between officers and enlisted men.

The present order is to be read to all companies, battalions, regiments, ships' crews, batteries, and other combatant and non-combatant commands.

The Petrograd Soviet of Workers' and Soldiers' Deputies

Vernadsky, *Source Book of Russian History*, vol. 3 (**10**), p. 882.

document 6
Germany's involvement in the Russian Revolution

[a] FINANCIAL SUPPORT

*From the beginning of the war the German foreign ministry had been aware of the possibility of using the Socialist movement as a means of weakening the Tsarist government, and in March 1915 Alexander Helphand (Parvus) offered to act as a link between it and the various groups in Russia (**69**). From then on the German government supplied millions of marks for the purpose of fomenting revolution there. Until 1917 the Bolsheviks seem to have received very little of this, but after Lenin's return to Petrograd they were in receipt of large sums through Helphand from his base at Copenhagen, and through Fürstenberg (Hanecki), an associate of Lenin's at Stockholm (see p. 33) (**43**, **59**). The following extract is from a telegram sent by the German foreign minister, von Kühlmann, to the army headquarters on 3 December 1917 (western dating).*

The disruption of the Entente and the subsequent creation of political combinations agreeable to us constitute the most important war aim of our diplomacy. Russia appeared to be the weakest link in the enemy chain, the task therefore was gradually to loosen it, and, when possible, to remove it. This was the purpose of the subversive activity we caused to be carried out in Russia behind the front – in the first place promotion of separatist tendencies and support of the Bolsheviks. It was not until the Bolsheviks had received from us a steady flow of funds through various channels and under different labels that they were in a position to be able to built up their main organ, *Pravda*, to conduct energetic propaganda and appreciably to extend the originally narrow basis of their party. The Bolsheviks have now come to power; how long they will retain power cannot be yet foreseen. They need peace in order to strengthen their own position; on the other hand, it is entirely in our interest that we should exploit the period while they are in power, which may be a short one, in order to attain firstly an armistice and then, if possible, peace.

[b] THE SEALED TRAIN

It was Helphand who suggested to the German government that they should provide facilities for Lenin's return to Russia through Germany by train, and Martov who put the idea to Lenin in Switzerland (see p. 31). In the hope of avoiding suspicions that he was a German agent, Lenin insisted that other non-Bolshevik Socialists should be included in the party, and that there should be no external contact during the journey through Germany. A Swiss Socialist, Fritz Platten, acted as courier. The following is a telegram from the German foreign minister, Zimmermann, to the German ambassador at Stockholm on 7 April 1917 (western dating).

A number of Russian revolutionaries in Switzerland (exact number not yet decided) is to be given permission to travel through Germany in order to return to Russia via Sweden. They will be accompanied by the secretary of the Swiss Social Democratic party, Platten. Provisionally, they will probably arrive at Sassnitz on Wednesday, 11 April.

Please make the necessary arrangements with the Swedish government, in confidence.

Report their attitude by telegram.

Zimmermann

Zeman, *Germany and the Revolution in Russia 1915–1918* (**11**), pp. 41, 94.

document 7
The withering away of the state

At the time of its writing Lenin clearly regarded his essay State and Revolution *as an important statement of doctrine. In the summer of 1917 he sent for the notes which he had deposited in Stockholm on his way to Russia and wrote most of it while hiding in Finland in September. It was not published until after the October revolution when events were already beginning to belie the optimistic visionary note that runs through it (see p. 69).*

Furthermore, during the transition from capitalism to Communism suppression is still necessary; but it is now the suppression of the exploiting minority by the exploited majority. A special apparatus, a special machine for suppression, the state, is still necessary, but it is now a transitory state; it is no longer a state in the proper sense; for the suppression of the minority of exploiters by the majority of the wage-slaves of yesterday is comparatively so easy, simple and natural a task that it will entail far less bloodshed than the suppression of the risings of slaves, serfs or wage-labourers, and it will cost mankind far less. And it is compatible with the extension of democracy to such an overwhelming majority of the population that the need for a special machine of suppression will begin to disappear. The exploiters are naturally unable to suppress the people without a very complex machine for performing this task; but the people can suppress the exploiters even with a very simple machine, almost without a machine, without a special apparatus, by the simple organization of the armed masses (such as the Soviets of Workers' and Soldiers' Deputies, we may remark, running ahead a little).

Finally, only Communism makes the state absolutely unnecessary, for there is nobody to be suppressed – 'nobody' in the sense of class, in the sense of a systematic struggle against a definite section of the population. We are not utopians, and we do not in the least deny the possibility and inevitability of excesses on the part of individual persons, or the need to suppress such excesses. But, in the first place, no special machine, no special apparatus of repression is needed for this; this will be done by the armed people itself, as simply and as readily as any crowd of civilized people, even in modern society, parts two people who are fighting, or interferes to prevent a woman from being assaulted. And, secondly, we know that the fundamental social cause of excesses, which consist of violating the rules of social intercourse, is the exploitation of the masses, their want and their poverty. With the removal of this chief cause, excesses will inevitably begin to 'wither away'. We do not know how quickly and in what order, but we know that they will wither away. With their withering away the state will also wither away.

Without indulging in utopias, Marx defined more fully what can be defined now regarding this future state, namely, the difference between the lower and higher phases (degrees, stages) of Communist society.

The Essentials of Lenin (**6**), vol. 2, pp. 202–203.

document 8
The decision for the October Revolution

At the meeting of the Bolshevik central committee on 10 October 1917 in Petrograd, Lenin was able to gain agreement over the projected coup (see p. 38). It is noticeable, however, that the resolution makes no mention of a date.

The Central Committee recognizes that the international position of the Russian revolution (the revolt in the German navy which is an extreme manifestation of the growth throughout Europe of the world Socialist revolution; the threat of the imperialist world with the object of strangling the revolution in Russia) as well as the military situation (the indubitable decision of the Russian bourgeoisie and Kerensky and Co. to surrender Petrograd to the Germans), and the fact that the proletarian party has gained a majority in the Soviets – all this, taken in conjunction with the peasant revolt and the swing of popular confidence towards our Party (the elections in Moscow), and, finally, the obvious preparations being made for a second Kornilov affair (the withdrawal of troops from Petrograd, the dispatch of Cossacks to Petrograd, the surrounding of Minsk by Cossacks, etc.) – all this places the armed uprising on the order of the day.

Considering therefore that an armed uprising is inevitable, and that the time for it is fully ripe, the Central Committee instructs all Party organizations to be guided accordingly, and to discuss and decide all practical questions (the Congress of Soviets of the Northern Region, the withdrawal of troops from Petrograd, the action of our people in Moscow and Minsk, etc.) from this point of view.

The Essentials of Lenin (**6**), vol. 2, p. 135.

document 9
Preparations for the Battle of Pulkovo

John Reed, a left-wing American journalist, was present in Petrograd during the October revolution, of which he wrote an enthusiastic account shortly afterwards. He died of typhus in Russia in 1920 and is buried in Red Square. This passage describes the haphazard organization of the Bolshevik defence against Kerensky's efforts to retake Petrograd a few days after the coup (see p. 42). Antonov and Dybenko, commissars for military and naval affairs, set out in the direction of Pulkovo, accompanied by Trusishka, a Russian acquaintance of Reed's.

As they went down the Suvorovsky Prospect, someone mentioned food. They might be out for three or four days, in a country indifferently well provisioned. They stopped the car. Money? The Commissar of War looked through his pockets. He hadn't a kopek. The Commissar of Marine was broke. So was the chauffeur. Trüsishka bought the provisions.

Just as they turned into the Nevsky a tyre blew out. [*Eventually they commandeered another car.*] Arrived at Narvskaya Zastava, about ten miles out, Antonov called for the commandant of the Red Guard. He was led to the edge of the town, where some few hundred workmen had dug trenches and were waiting for the Cossacks.

"Everything all right here, comrade?" asked Antonov.

"Everything perfect, comrade," answered the commandant. "The troops are in excellent spirits. . . . Only one thing – we have no ammunition. . . ."

"In Smolny there are two billion rounds," Antonov told him. "I will give you an order." He felt in his pockets. "Has anyone a piece of paper?"

Dybenko had none – nor the couriers. Trusishka had to offer his note-book. . . .

"Devil! I have no pencil!" cried Antonov. "Who's got a pencil?" Needless to say, Trusishka had the only pencil in the crowd.

Reed, *Ten Days That Shook The World* (**22**), pp. 172–173.

The Cheka's orders to the Soviets

document 10

This order was issued on 22 February 1918 and was published in Pravda *on the following day (see p. 53).*

The All-Russian Extraordinary Commission to Fight Counter-Revolution, Sabotage and Speculation asks the [local] Soviets to proceed at once to seek out, arrest and shoot immediately all members . . . connected in one form or another with counter-revolutionary organizations . . . (1) agents of enemy spies,

(2) counter-revolutionary agitators, (3) speculators, (4) organizers of revolts . . . against the Soviet government, (5) those going to the Don to join the Kaledin-Kornilov band and the Polish counter-revolutionary legions, (6) buyers and sellers of arms to be used by the counter-revolutionary bourgeoisie – all these are to be shot on the spot . . . when caught red handed in the act.

The All-Russian Cheka

Bunyan & Fisher, *The Bolshevik Revolution 1917–1918* (**1**), p. 576.

document 11
The acceptance of the Peace of Brest-Litovsk

After the signing of the peace on 3 March 1918 Lenin still had to fight for its acceptance. In this speech at the seventh Bolshevik party congress on 6 March he stressed the improbability of an immediate revolution in central Europe, the very reverse of the argument that he had used on 10 October (see p. 52). The second paragraph is clearly aimed at Bukharin and the Left Communists.

It will be a good thing if the German proletariat will be able to come out. But have you measured, have you discovered such an instrument, one that will determine that the German revolution will break out on such and such a day? No, that you do not know, and neither do we. You are staking everything on this card. If the revolution breaks out, everything is saved. Of course. But if it does not turn out as we desire, supposing it does not achieve victory tomorrow – what then? Then the masses will say to you: you acted like gamblers – you staked everything on a fortunate turn of events that did not take place, you proved unfit for the situation that actually arose in place of an international revolution, which will inevitably come, but which has not ripened yet.

A period has set in of severe defeats, inflicted by imperialism, armed to the teeth, upon a country which has demobilized its army, which had to demobilize. What I foretold has come to pass; instead of the Brest-Litovsk peace we have received a much more humiliating peace, and the blame for this rests upon those who refused to accept the former peace.

The Essentials of Lenin (**6**) vol. 2, p. 302

document 12
The debate over state capitalism

A conference of Bolshevik leaders on 4 April 1918 clearly illustrated the divide between Lenin and the Left Communists over industrial organization (see p. 48).

[a] *Lenin was emphatic that the state must take control of the development of industry and, as a temporary measure, make use of bourgeois managers and specialists.*

Without the guidance of specialists in the different branches of science, technology, and experience, no transition to socialism is possible, because as compared with capitalism socialism requires a deliberate and forward mass movement toward higher productivity of labour . . . But the majority of the specialists are bourgeois. . . . Many of these saboteurs "go to their jobs," but the best organizers and the biggest specialists can be utilized by the state either in the old, bourgeois way (i.e. for high salaries) or in the new, proletarian way (i.e. by instituting a regime of all-inclusive accounting and control which would automatically subordinate and enlist the specialists for our work).

For the present we shall have to adopt the old bourgeois method and agree to pay very high salaries for the "services" of the biggest bourgeois specialists. All who are familiar with the situation see the necessity of such a measure, though not all understand its significance for the proletarian state. Clearly it is a compromise measure, a departure from the principles of the Paris Commune. . . .

The Russians are bad workers as compared with the advanced nations. It could not have been otherwise under the Tsarist regime with the system of slavery still alive. To learn how to work is a problem which the Soviet power must place before the people in all its significance. The last word of capitalism in that respect – the Taylor system – is, like every other capitalist improvement, a combination of the most refined brutality of capitalist exploitation with the richest scientific gains. This is achieved by analyzing the mechanical movements of a worker at his task, by eliminating superfluous awkward motions, by elaborating the best processes of work, by introducing the best system of accounting, control, etc.

The Soviet Republic must at any cost adopt everything that is valuable in the conquests of science and technology . . . The realization of socialism will be determined precisely by our success in combining the Soviet power and Soviet organization of administration with the most up-to-date progress of capitalism. It is necessary to introduce into Russia the study and teaching of the Taylor system. . . .

[b] *In the following extract the Left Communists stated their objections to Lenin's policy.*

Instead of leading from partial nationalization to complete social-ization of large-scale industry, agreements with "captains of industry" would lead to the formation of large trusts controlled by the latter and embracing all basic branches of industry. The trusts, to be sure, would be given the appearance of government under-takings. Such a system of organizing production would provide a social basis for evolution toward state capitalism and would be but a transition to it.

The policy of organizing the management of [industrial] enter-prises on a centralized and semi-bureaucratic basis and of permit-ting capitalists to participate widely in that management would naturally be bound up with the labour policy, which would aim to introduce among workers discipline under the guise of "self-discipline", labour duty for workers (such a project had already been proposed by the Right-Wing Bolsheviks), a piece-work system of wages, longer hours of labour, etc.

Government would have to become more bureaucratic and centralized, and individual commissars more dominant. Local Soviets would have to be deprived of their independence and the type of "commune-state" governed from below would have to be abandoned. Numerous facts go to indicate that there is already a definite tendency in this direction.

Bunyan & Fisher, *The Bolshevik Revolution 1917–1918* (1), pp. 555–6, 559, 561–2.

document 13
The victims

The following extract from Countess Sollohub's memoirs describes a scene that took place in the spring of 1920. Her husband had recently been killed fighting with the Whites in the south; her house in Petrograd and her estates had all been confiscated, and for three weeks she had been held on unspecified charges in the Lubianka and Butyrki prisons in Moscow. After her release she had returned to the Butyrki prison where she stood in a queue for seven hours waiting to deliver a parcel to a Catholic priest who was still confined there.

Hushed conversations were carried on here and there, but as soon as a voice became louder, a warder in uniform appeared and ordered silence. A few steps before me a young woman apparently belonging to the upper classes, poorly but neatly dressed, stood leaning wearily against the wall. She had struck me by the pallor of her face and the anxious expression of her large blue eyes. She exchanged a few short rapid sentences with her neighbours, but did not seem inclined to gossip.

Slowly step by step we progressed and came nearer to the barred end of the passage where the parcels were delivered. I dreaded the moment when it would be my turn to give the parcels, to name the prisoners they were intended for, to give my own name and address. I had the feeling that the warders and the women who ran the service would surely recognize me and would wonder why I should come now to help other prisoners and I feared above all that the mention of a Catholic priest would make me the more suspect. But I had undertaken to deliver the parcels and I had to do it. With a faint feeling in my heart I approached the rough wooden wall. Its fresh boards still smelt of the forest. . . . My thoughts were interrupted by a loud sob and harsh voices. I looked up and saw the young woman I had watched, leaning now against these boards, her eyes still larger, her lips white. I heard her say in an entreating voice to the woman warder who was receiving the parcels behind the counter: "Please, I implore you, do try to find out where my husband is. I looked for him in every prison in Moscow. I was here the other day; I was sent back everywhere with no reply. My only hope is that he may be here after all – do tell me."

The woman behind the counter was shrugging her shoulders impatiently, and leaning forward, was shouting now: "How can I know where your husband is? He may be shot long ago, or perhaps he was shot only this morning. How can I know? When parcels are not accepted, it means that they are of no use any more, that's clear. For all I know, your husband must have been shot, but it is none of our business to tell people who is shot and where and when he was shot." And on and on she went, juggling with this word "shot", throwing it at the young woman who stared now aghast, speechless. And in the heat of this cruel game the woman warder forgot her duty; she took mechanically my parcels, looked absentmindedly at the attached labels and never asked me for any details or for my own name and address. I stepped aside, people pushed on from behind, the young woman was making her way towards the door and I lost sight of her in the crowd.

Countess Edith Sollohub: *Private papers.*

document 14

Results of land socialization

This report was made by an official of the Commissariat of Agriculture for the period 1917–1920.

Socialization of land was not carried out on a national scale. The transformation of Russia into an all-embracing commune with frequent redistribution of land on the basis of equality, contemplated in the programmes of the Social Revolutionaries, could not be realised. In practice the land was simply appropriated by the local peasants, and no attempt was made on their part to migrate from places where land was scarce to those having it in greater abundance. Equal distribution of land inside a village took place everywhere, but equalization between volosts was less frequent. Still less frequent were the cases of equal distribution between uezds and gubernia.

Having got the land . . . the well-to-do peasant class seems to have attained its aim. But the results . . . of the partition were much less significant than was expected. The enormous amount of land, when distributed among many millions, gave most unsatisfactory results. A special investigation of the central office of the Land Department established the fact that the increase of area per capita in some places would be expressed in infinitesimal figures: tenths and even hundredths, of a desiatin [1.09 hectares]. In the majority of the gubernia that increase did not exceed half a desiatin.

Bunyan & Fisher, *The Bolshevik Revolution 1917–1918* (**1**), pp. 678–9.

document 15

New Economic Policy

This decree of the All-Russian Soviet Executive Committee was published in Pravda *on 23 March 1921 (see p. 62).*

In order to assure an efficient and untroubled economic life on the basis of a freer use by the farmer of the products of his labour and of his economic resources, in order to strengthen the peasant economy and raise its productivity and also in order to calculate precisely the obligation to the state which falls on the peasants, requisitioning, as a means of state collection of food supplies, raw material and fodder, is to be replaced by a tax in kind. . . .

2. This tax must be less than what the peasant has given up to this time through requisitions. The sum of the tax must be reckoned so as to cover the most essential needs of the army, the city workers, the non-agricultural population. The general sum of the tax must be diminished in as much as the re-establishment of transportation and industry will permit the Soviet government to receive agricultural products in exchange for factory and hand-industry products.

3. The tax is to be taken in the form of a percentage or partial deduction from the products raised in the peasant holding, taking into account the harvest, the number of eaters in the holding and the number of cattle.

4. The tax must be progressive; the percentage must be lower for the holdings of middle class and poorer peasants and of town workers. The holdings of the poorest peasants may be exempted from some and, in exceptional cases, from all forms of the tax in kind . . .

8. All the reserves of food, raw material and fodder which remain with the peasants after the tax has been paid are at their full disposition and may be used by them for improving and strengthening their holdings, for increasing personal consumption and for exchange for products of factory and hand-industry and of agriculture.

Exchange is permitted within the limits of local economic turnover, both through cooperative organization and through markets.

9. Those farmers who wish to deliver to the state the surplus in their possession after the tax has been paid must receive, in exchange for the voluntary delivery of this surplus, objects of general consumption and agricultural machinery. With this end in view, a steady state reserve fund of agricultural machinery and of objects of general consumption is being created. It includes both domestic products and goods purchased abroad. Part of the state gold reserve and part of the ready raw material are set aside for the purpose of making purchases abroad.

Chamberlin, *The Russian Revolution 1917–1921* (**54**) vol. 2, pp. 499–500.

Bibliography

ORIGINAL DOCUMENTS

1   Bunyan, J. and Fisher, H. H. *The Bolshevik Revolution 1917–1918*, Stanford University Press, 1934.
2   Bunyan, J. *Intervention, Civil War and Communism in Russia, April–December 1918*, Baltimore, 1936.
3   Gankin, O. H. and Fisher, H. H. *The Bolsheviks and the World War*, Stanford, 1940.
4   Kerensky, A. F. and Browder, R. P. *The Russian Provisional Government 1917*, Stanford, 1961.
5   Lenin, V. I. *What Is To Be Done?*, ed. Utechin, S. V. and P., Oxford, 1963.
6   *The Essentials of Lenin*, 2 vols., Lawrence and Wishart, 1947.
7   Luxemburg, Rosa. *The Russian Revolution*, and *Leninism or Marxism?* Michigan, 1970.
8   McCauley, M., ed. *The Russian Revolution and the Soviet State, 1917–1921: Documents*, Weidenfeld and Nicolson, 1976.
9   Woodward, E. L. and Butler, R., eds. *Documents on British Foreign Policy 1919–1939*, 1st series, H.M.S.O.
10 Vernadsky, G. *et al.*, *A Source Book of Russian History*, vol. 3, Yale University Press, 1972.
11 Zeman, Z. A. B., ed. *Germany and the Revolution in Russia 1915–1918*, Oxford, 1958.
12 *The Essential Left* (including *The Communist Manifesto* and Lenin's *State and Revolution*), Allen and Unwin, 1960.

MEMOIRS

13 Buchanan, Sir George. *My Mission to Russia*, 2 vols., Cassell, 1923.
14 Denikin, General A. I. *The Russian Turmoil*, Hutchinson, 1922.
15 Denikin, General A. I. *The White Army*, Cape, 1930.
16 Kerensky, A. F. *The Kerensky Memoirs*, Cassell, 1966.
17 Knox, Major General Sir Alfred. *With the Russian Army*, 2 vols., Hutchinson, 1921.
18 Lockhart, Bruce. *Memoirs of a British Agent*, Putnam, 1932.

Bibliography

19 Price, M. Phillips. *Reminiscences of the Russian Revolution*, London, 1921.

20 Ransome, A. *Six Weeks in Russia in 1919*, Allen and Unwin, 1919.

21 Ransome, A. *Autobiography*, Cape, 1976.

22 Reed, J. *Ten Days That Shook The World*, Penguin, 1966.

23 Sukhanov, N. *The Russian Revolution 1917*, ed. Carmichael, J. Oxford, 1955.

24 Trotsky, L. *My Life*, Penguin, 1975.

BACKGROUND OF THOUGHT

25 Berdyaev, N. *The Origin of Russian Communism*, G. Bles, 1937.

26 Berlin, I. *Karl Marx*, Oxford, 1939.

27 Carew Hunt, R. N. *The Theory and Practice of Communism*, G. Bles, 1950.

28 Cole, G. D. H. *History of Socialist Thought*, vol. 4, Macmillan, 1958.

29 Haimson, L. T. *The Russian Marxists and the Origins of Bolshevism*, Harvard University Press, 1955.

30 Hare, R. *Pioneers of Russian Social Thought*, Oxford, 1951.

31 Hare, R. *Portraits of Russian Personalities*, Oxford, 1959.

32 Joll, J. *The Second International*, Weidenfeld and Nicolson, 1955.

33 Joll, J. *The Anarchists*, Eyre and Spottiswoode, 1964.

34 Keep, J. L. H. *The Rise of Social Democracy in Russia*, Oxford, 1963.

35 Lichtheim, G. *A Short History of Socialism*, Weidenfeld and Nicolson, 1970.

36 McLellan, D. *Karl Marx: his Life and Thought*, Macmillan, 1973.

37 Plamenatz, J. *German Marxism and Russian Communism*, Longman, 1954.

38 Szamuely, T. *The Russian Tradition*, Secker and Warburg, 1974.

39 Treadgold, D. W. *Lenin and his rivals*, Methuen, 1955.

40 Venturi, F. *Roots of Revolution*, Weidenfeld and Nicolson, 1960.

41 Weeks, A. L. *First Bolshevik: Peter Tkachev*, New York, 1968.

PRE-1917

42 Falkus, M. E. *The Industrialization of Russia 1700–1914*, Macmillan, 1972.

43 Futrell, M. *Northern Underground*, Faber, 1963.

44 Harcave, S. *First Blood: The Russian Revolution of 1905*, Bodley Head, 1964.

45 Hosking, G. A. *The Russian Constitutional Experiment 1907–1914*, Cambridge, 1973.

46 Kindersley, R. *The First Russian Revisionists*, Oxford, 1962.

47 Pearson, R. *The Russian Moderates and the Crisis of Tsarism 1914–17*, Macmillan, 1977.

48 Pipes, R. *Social Democracy and the St. Petersburg Labour Movement 1885–1897*, Harvard University Press, 1963.

49 Schwarz, S. M. *The Revolution of 1905*, University of Chicago, 1967.

50 Seton Watson, H. *The Decline of Imperial Russia 1855–1914*, Methuen, 1952.

51 Stone, N. *The Eastern Front 1914–1917*, Hodder and Stoughton, 1975.

52 Wallace, Sir Donald Mackenzie. *Russia on the Eve of War and Revolution*, Random House Inc., 1961.

POLITICAL HISTORIES

53 Carr, E. H. *The Bolshevik Revolution 1917–1923*, 3 vols., Penguin, 1966.

54 Chamberlin, W. H. *The Russian Revolution 1917–1921*, 2 vols., Macmillan, 1935.

55 Ferro, M. *The Russian Revolution of February 1917*, Routledge and Kegan Paul, 1972.

56 Ferro, M. *October 1917*, Routledge and Kegan Paul, 1980.

57 Fitzpatrick, S. *The Russian Revolution*, Oxford University Press, 1982.

58 Hasegawa, T. *The February Revolution: Petrograd, 1917*, University of Washington Press, 1981.

59 Katkov, G. *Russia 1917: The February Revolution*, Longman, 1967.

60 Keep, J. L. H. *The Russian Revolution: a Study in Mass Mobilization*, Weidenfeld and Nicolson, 1976.

61 Kennan, G. *Soviet-American Relations 1917–1920*, 2 vols., Faber, 1956, 1958.

62 Liebman, M. *The Russian Revolution*, Cape, 1970.

63 McCauley, M. *The Soviet Union since 1917*, Longman, 1981.

64 Rabinowitch, A. *Prelude to Revolution. The Petrograd Bolsheviks and the July 1917 Uprising*, Indiana University Press, 1968.

65 Rabinowitch, A. *The Bolsheviks Come To Power*, Norton, New York, 1976.

66 Schapiro, L. *The Origin of the Communist Autocracy*, Macmillan, 1955.

Bibliography

67 Schapiro, L. *The Communist Party of the Soviet Union*, Methuen, 1970.

68 Trotsky, L. *The Russian Revolution*, Gollancz, 1932–33.

BIOGRAPHIES
(*alphabetically by subject*)

69 Zeman, Z. A. B. and Scharlau, W. B. *The Merchant of Revolution: A. I. Helphand*, Oxford, 1965.

70 Deutscher, I. *Lenin's Childhood*, Oxford, 1970.

71 Possony, S. T. *Lenin, the Compulsive Revolutionary*, Allen and Unwin, 1966.

72 Shub, D. *Lenin*, Pelican, 1966.

73 Shukman, H. *Lenin and the Russian Revolution*, Batsford, 1967.

74 Ulam, A. B. *Lenin and the Bolsheviks*, Secker and Warburg, 1966.

75 Getzler, I. *Martov*, Cambridge, 1967.

76 Baron, S. H. *Plekhanov: the Father of Russian Marxism*, Routledge and Kegan Paul, 1963.

77 Deutscher, I. *Stalin*, Oxford, 1949.

78 Ulam, A. B. *Stalin*, Secker and Warburg, 1966.

79 Carmichael, J. *Trotsky*, Hodder and Stoughton, 1975.

80 Deutscher, I. *Trotsky*, vol. 1, *The Prophet Armed 1879–1921*, Oxford, 1954.

81 Deutscher, I. *Trotsky*, vol. 2, *The Prophet Unarmed 1921–1929*, Oxford, 1959.

82 Deutscher, I. *Trotsky*, vol. 3, *The Prophet Outcast 1929–1940*, Oxford, 1970.

83 Wolfe, B. D. *Three who Made a Revolution*, Pelican, 1966.

PARTICULAR SUBJECTS

84 Carsten, F. *Revolution in Central Europe 1918–1919*, Temple Smith, 1972.

85 Dobb, M. *Soviet Economic Development since 1917*, Routledge and Kegan Paul, 1948.

86 Footman, D. *Civil War in Russia*, Faber, 1961.

87 Katkov, G. *Russia 1917: The Kornilov Affair*, Longman, 1980.

88 Luckett, R. *The White Generals*, Longman, 1971.

89 Mandel, D. *The Petrograd Workers and the Fall of the Old Regime*, Macmillan, 1983.

90 Pares, B. *The Fall of the Russian Monarchy*, Cape, 1939.

91 Radkey, O. H. *The Agrarian Foes of Bolshevism*, Columbia University Press, 1958.

92 Radkey, O. H. *Sickle under the Hammer*, Columbia University Press, 1963.

93 Selznick, P. *The Organizational Weapon*, McGraw-Hill Book Company, 1952.

94 Smith, S. *Red Petrograd*, Cambridge University Press, 1983.

95 Wheeler-Bennett, J. W. *Brest-Litovsk: The Forgotten Peace*, Macmillan, 1938.

96 Wildman, A. K. *The End of the Russian Imperial Army*, Princeton University Press, 1980.

97 Zeman, Z. A. B. *The Break-up of the Habsburg Empire 1914–1918*, Oxford, 1961.

98 St. Antony's Papers No. 6: *Soviet Affairs*, Chatto and Windus, 1959. No. 12: *Soviet Affairs*, Chatto and Windus, 1962.

99 *Revolutionary Russia*, ed. R. Pipes, Harvard University Press, 1968.

Index

Index